The Lost Ships

An Adventure in Undersea Archaeology

~~~~~~~~~~~~~~~~~~~~~~~~~~~~~~~~~~~~~

BY Peter Throckmorton

WITH ILLUSTRATIONS

An Atlantic Monthly Press Book

LITTLE, BROWN AND COMPANY · BOSTON · TORONTO

ATLANTIC–LITTLE, BROWN BOOKS
ARE PUBLISHED BY
LITTLE, BROWN AND COMPANY
IN ASSOCIATION WITH
THE ATLANTIC MONTHLY PRESS

*Published simultaneously in Canada
by Little, Brown & Company (Canada) Limited*

PRINTED IN THE UNITED STATES OF AMERICA

This book is for Virginia Grace

Acknowledgments

I WISH to express my gratitude first of all to those people who helped me in 1958 and 1959 in Turkey, especially Osman Nuri Bilgin, educational director of Bodrum; Mustafa Kapkin, Rasim Divanli, Hakki Gultekin, John Huston of the Council of Underwater Archaeology, Virginia Grace of the American School of Classical Studies, the sponge divers of Bodrum, and most of all Captain Kemal Arras.

I am also indebted to James Dugan, without whose advice and encouragement I should not have written *Lost Ships;* Edward A. McCreary and Malcolm Douglas, who made it possible for me to return to Bodrum in 1960; William Garrett of the National Geographic Society; Henry Chapin, who read the manuscript in progress; and especially to Joan Henley Potok, who typed the manuscript, for her invaluable editorial help.

Contents

(Illustrations appear between pages 118 and 119)

CONTENTS

The Lost Ships

~~~~~

Introduction

I saw my first sunken ship at the bottom of Honolulu harbor. She was a wooden minesweeper which had been abandoned, to sink slowly when the shipworms weakened her planking. The water was dirty, and I could not see far. I was using the cable that held the marker buoy to the wreck as a descending line. It was overgrown with glutinous, unsavory globs of green seaweed, under which grew razor-sharp mussels. I was afraid.

I reached the mast and worked my way carefully past tangled rigging. The ship, still invisible, made itself felt as a dark presence looming below. The bridge came into sight. The pilothouse windows gaped like eyeholes in a skull, the darkness behind them concealing unimaginable terrors. Avoiding the bridge, I worked my way down the little ship's side. She was canted over to starboard; I found the overhang ominous. Her bronze screws gleamed above the black slime of the bottom, which was littered with rotting cardboard and rusty beer cans.

I swam up to the main deck. The messroom door hung agape. Although the interior was dark, a dim rectangle of light showed that the door which led to the deck on the other side of the ship was open. My companion saw me hesitating and swam coolly past me through the door and out the other side. I pulled myself together and followed him. There was nothing inside but a rusty coffee urn.

But I had been caught by something harder to kill than any of the fabled beasts that storytellers put in sunken ships, stronger even than the giant groupers which inhabit wrecks in some tropical waters. That minesweeper crystallized the interest in shipwrecks which I had always had, and my interest in seamen, ships, and voyages.

As a child I had devoured everything that I could find in print about shipwrecks. My mother kept my first composition, which concluded, "The ship sunk everybody drownded. Flotsam and jetsam litered the water." I didn't know what flotsam and jetsam were, and I pronounced them flotSAM and jetSAM, but I could spell them, and I wanted some.

I was ten years old when the great hurricane of 1938 covered the beaches of Long Island with pieces of smashed yachts and fishing boats. With an instinct for salvage as unerring and unreasoning as a pack rat's gathering of glitter, I collected tons of nautical debris and piled it in the yard of the house where I was spending the summer.

With the help of a friend, I salvaged the ownerless

hulk of a sailing boat which was rotting in the shallows. We cut up our bedsheets for sails. When our mothers forbade us the boat, we stripped it of its bronze fittings, and loaded it with a cargo of stones, which we pretended were silver bars. We paddled the boat to deep water and had a memorable game of pirates which culminated with our boarding and sinking it after an imaginary battle during which we slew hecatombs of make-believe Spaniards. Using goggles which made everything look cross-eyed, we dived to admire the wreck.

The sea was the only fixed thing in my childhood, for my parents were divorced when I was very small, and I divided my time between them and the boarding schools and summer camps where I was sent from the time I was seven. To this day I cannot clearly say where I am from, except that every peregrination ended in New York, where I was born, and that I feel strongly that I am not from Chicago, where my father settled because of his job with a manufacturing company. Perhaps the prospect of another summer mucking manure on my father's "farm" was what drove me to run away to sea before I finished school.

The navy rejected me because of weak eyes. I hoboed my way across America, worked around a dozen seaports on barges and fishing boats. I shipped out in a tanker, signed off six months later in Honolulu, and went to work in a junkyard.

The war was over and the armed services began selling surplus material by the ton. A typical "lot" might contain two trucks, ten thousand gas masks, and a heap of boxes of engine parts identified only by illegible code numbers. The trick lay in bidding no more than the real value of what you knew you could sell. The profit was in the unmarked boxes. One lot contained tons of heavy diving gear, which lay in a corner of the warehouse for months until it was purchased by a drunken ex-navy diver named Charley, who was setting up in business on his own. He promised to teach me to dive.

I went to work for the diver, and he kept his promise, but then he went broke and I was left high and dry. Charley swore that he was my father and signed the papers for my enlistment into the Army Transportation Corps, which eventually put me to work in a Yokohama shipyard.

I was crazy about diving, but army regulations forbade us to dive. I made friends with the shipyard divers. We drydocked ships several times a month. Adjusting keelblocks after the ship was in the dock usually took place the night before the dock was pumped out, when there were seldom any officers around. Writing fifteen years later, it is hard to remember why it was fun diving in a Jap helmet diving rig a foot too short for me, in the wintertime, in total darkness.

But Yokohama was a wonderful place to be if you liked ships. During the day I worked on big ships. At night and on weekends I worked on or sailed my own small boat. I got myself transferred to a fireboat which was based on an island in the bay between Tokyo and Yokohama, and spent the long watches studying so that I could go to college when I was released from the service.

I was fascinated by the Japanese, especially by the sea people of Tokyo bay. A friendly anthropologist took me on as temporary assistant in his archaeological investigations of the Japanese neolithic period. I had not enough background to do very useful work, but the experience made me determined to study.

In due course I was paid off in Honolulu, after four years in the army, and enrolled at the University of Hawaii. It was the year the aqualung came on the market. Those who dive for the first time with the aqualung can never know what the device meant to those of us who underwent our diving apprenticeship in helmet diving gear. As it was designed to do by Captain Cousteau, the aqualung frees man in the sea. A device which simplifies diving to the essentials, it allows the diver to breathe, by means of a regulator, compressed air from bottles strapped to his back. The standard navy diving suit is of course an admirable device, more suitable for some kinds of work than the aqualung. But it is much more expensive, and the diver requires a boat above him and skillful attention from a minimum of two tenders before its use is safe.

Like most students on the GI bill at the University of Hawaii, I was perpetually broke. I discovered that people would pay to see divers perform underwater, and spent my afternoons under a glass-bottomed boat, catching octopuses with my bare hands and spearing moray eels while tourists stared. After that first encounter with the many-doored minesweeper, I spent my spare time hunting wrecks. Scrap bronze bought me a sports car, and speared fish paid the rent. I acquired an interest in a hundred-ton fishing boat, a truck, a huge barge, and a bank account. My partner bought a tugboat.

Soon I had no time to study, and no time to dive. I was becoming a businessman. I had wanted the wild world; the sea was a key to this. Then I had wanted to learn strange languages and understand distant people, to camp by the tents of Shinar, sail in copra schooners, and smell spices in Zanzibar. Instead, I was stuck in a provincial town in the middle of the Pacific Ocean.

I was twenty-five when I was accepted as a candidate for a higher degree in ethnology at the Museum of Man in Paris. My GI bill ran out there a year later. I lumped cabbages every night until I found a job as assistant to a documentary-film maker, and took up free-lance photography at the same time. It was a wild and wonderful existence, and one day I just stopped going to school.

I worked my way across the old world, doing my bit to satisfy the greedy public's desire for photographs of royal weddings, revolutions, murders, accidents, and the adventures and amours of film stars. I saw some spectacular sights. I was still boat-crazy, but there was no future for me at sea, unless someday I could afford a small sailing boat. I planned dozens of nautical assignments and proposed them to editors, who inevitably found work for me inland.

In the spring of 1958 four of us were driving across Afghanistan toward Europe, after a winter's filming in India. A few miles past Herat, halfway across a dry river bed, the battered French Ford stuck. We got out and pushed. The wheels spun. The car settled slowly onto her axles.

We had been in Central Asia for a month, and were tired. Our insides ached with dysentery. Worse than sickness was the *cafard* we shared. We were tired of each other, the endless steppes, the flat tires, the disintegrating car. We stank. Our leader, Jean Naz, a weary grin splitting his dust-grayed fox face, gestured and with just the right tone of voice got us out again to push. In the middle of it all the wind began to howl and a yellow

[8]

cloud covered the sun. The temperature rose ten degrees, and we found ourselves in a sandstorm, a real one, the kind that buries caravans forever. We crawled into the car and tried to breathe, while the sand blasted the closed windows.

"There are places where the water is so clear that you hang on to the boat for fear of falling." It was J. J. Flori, lately cameraman on *Calypso*, the famous research vessel from which Captain Cousteau had launched free diving. Like me, he was a passionate diver. He did not look like a diver now, hunched in a corner of the back seat. His scruffy head sprouted out of the disintegrating folds of an erstwhile eiderdown jacket like a badger emerging from its den. His cracked lips moved like little animals in the undergrowth of his dirty beard. My attention would not have been caught so surely if I had not been expecting a curse when he whispered softly: "The sea, Peter, do you remember the sea?"

For a moment I held back, and then gave myself up to the old dream of the cool and faultless sea. We talked of coral gardens, the habits of sharks in the Society Islands, and of wrecks.

The storm ended. We dug ourselves out of the sand and drove on. Eventually we came to the pass in the mountains over Trebizond where Xenophon, riding in the rear, heard a commotion up ahead and, fearing another attack by the natives, galloped to the head of the pass to discover his men shouting:

"The sea, the sea!"

In Istanbul I found myself alone and at loose ends after a winter of steady employment. The others had gone on to Paris. First I heard that a beautiful bronze

bust of Demeter had been found near a place called
Bodrum in southern Turkey. Then I was told about a
Turkish diver-photographer who lived in Izmir, the
main port of Aegean Turkey. His name was Mustafa
Kapkin, and he was glad to see me.

Mustafa was a slight man, black-haired and olive-
skinned, with liquid brown eyes. He was full of funny
stories and charming turns of speech in English, which
he spoke badly, and German, which he spoke well. He
had flown fighters in the Turkish Air Force, and his
mannerisms were still those of a fighter pilot. Unlike
most Turks, he was gay. This perhaps was because his
family came to Izmir from Crete as refugees of the
Balkan wars in 1912. He always spoke Greek with his
mother, because she had never learned to speak Turkish
well. It was not until I came to Greece that I understood
that he was neither Turkish nor Greek, but Cretan. In
short, he was a sea person, of the basic stock of the
Aegean sea people.

Mustafa was prospering as a commercial photographer, and his work had taken him all over Aegean Turkey. Like me, he was fascinated by sponge divers,
wrecks, and the sea. It was getting hot in Izmir and
springtime was never very busy anyhow. We decided to
go to Bodrum.

Since it was impossible then to import diving equipment into Turkey because of currency restrictions, we
collected some gear which had been copied from com-
mercially manufactured equipment. We intended to
meet some sponge divers, and to attempt to find out
exactly where the Demeter had come from. It might,
we thought, make a good article. We didn't really care.
I was happy to be out of Asia, following the dream of

clear water that had possessed me since the day of the sandstorm. Mustafa was glad to escape for a while from the heat of Izmir and the daily round of his work. Like Xenophon — the literary gentleman of Athens who accepted a friend's invitation to come along on an interesting adventure and a few months later found himself leading ten thousand men across Asia — I didn't know what I was getting into.

I

~~~~~

Pots in the Sea

One shoal, about 2 cable lengths off the
S.W. island, is the only danger in the whole
cluster, which may be traversed in every direction . . .

<div align="right">Captain Beaufort's Survey of 1811</div>

AFTER TWELVE HOURS cramped among the chickens
in the country bus, we came out of the last piny
mountain valley and saw Bodrum spread out below us.
We had come in at the top of a huge natural amphitheater. The town lay where the stage should be. Its
backdrop was the blue Aegean with a scattering of hazy
islands. A huge castle, with a red Turkish flag flying
from the keep, dominated the village and the sea beyond. We found rooms in the little hotel, deposited our
baggage, and headed for the waterfront to find some of
the divers and captains known to Mustafa from his trip
to Bodrum the year before.

Impressive from the heights above the town, the castle was overpowering from the waterfront. I found the
ramp which led into the looming walls past a whitewashed police station, went through a first gate, crossed
a dry moat, and found myself in a court half the size of a

football field. The crenellated walls of the great keep cut off the evening light. I saw a stair leading up and climbed it, passing coats of arms cut into marble blocks high in the walls. I came to a narrow gate, half closed by a rotten wooden door which hung askew from the one rusty hinge. The lintel seemed to have been the architrave of a classical building. Engraved on it was:

I.H.S. SALVA NOS DOMINE VIGILANTES
NISI DOMINUS CUSTODIERIT CIVITATEM
FRUSTRA VIGILAT QUI CUSTODIT EAM.

It was almost dark. I went under the gate, thinking that the Latin had an echo of my own childhood in it: "Jesus save us, guard our sleep." This was a Christian castle, and the fact that I was a Christian in Turkey came suddenly home. My own people had built this castle, not so long ago, as things went in Turkey.

I wandered into the central bailey, with *salva nos* ringing in my ears. It was almost too dark to see. There was a grunt and a rattle of stones. Two shapeless forms rushed by in the half-light. I started in cold terror, whispered "Salva nos," and laughed when I recognized the forms as mules, pastured there.

I picked my way back through fallen stones. At the gate I heard the wail of a tuneless Turkish song distorted by a loudspeaker, and followed it to a cafe, where I found Mustafa already practicing his gift of finding friends wherever he might be.

He was sitting with a man whom he introduced as Ahmet Kaptan. About thirty-five, Ahmet might have been handsome a few years before. Now his nose was red-veined from too much drinking, and his hands were shaky. There were food stains on the red and white checked shirt which he wore over a thick wool sweater, like all the other men in the cafe. (I wondered how they stood it. I had on only a sport shirt and I was burning up.) Like every other adult male in Bodrum, Ahmet Kaptan needed a shave. He was proud of being singled out by Mustafa. It marked him as a man of the world to sit with the voyagers from far away, and to exchange a few words of amiable but mutually unintelligible pidgin Italian with me, under the admiring gaze of the villagers.

After an exchange in which the most intimate details of my personal life were extracted, discussed, and filed away in village memories, we ordered a dinner of shish kebab, peppers with yogurt and rice, and half a liter of raki, the Turkish national drink. It is rather like anisette, with a licorice taste, turns white when you add water, and is deceptively smooth. After the third shot, the captain began to talk. He had quit diving, and had turned his sponge boat into a cargo carrier. The sponge business was rotten; plastic sponges were killing the market. The captain who had found the Demeter was at sea.

Did our captain know of any other wrecks? Yes, he had seen several. From his description, I knew that he was talking about modern wrecks. I got Mustafa to ask if he had ever seen any pots in the sea.

"Like that?" Ahmet Kaptan pointed to the amphora which held the drinking water in the corner of the restaurant. Why, the sea was stiff with pots! Some areas were so full of them that trawlers and sponge draggers had a hard time working.

I leaned forward, fascinated. We were interrupted by

a man who had come in five minutes before and sat down a few feet away. He had been staring at me ever since, as if I were an apparition from Mars. He finally got up enough courage to ask who or what I was. Mustafa told him that I was an American. He nodded with evident approval and concentrated on my features, as if he were trying to discover the secret of the universe in the reflections from my eyeglasses. Ahmet Kaptan began to talk politics, while I tried to get Mustafa to ask him about all those pots. As people came into the cafe, the strange man stopped them and pointed toward me.

"*Americalar, Americalar.*" They would nod with what appeared to be approval and interest, and sit down for a good stare themselves. I tried to appear unconcerned, and listened while Mustafa translated and Ahmet Kaptan told us how it was standard practice for trawlermen to smash amphoras and other things that came up in the nets "so they cannot tear the nets again," and how, only a week before, a friend of his had brought up and smashed over fifty in one day.

Had he heard of piles of pots in the sea? "Piles of pots in the sea! Why, only a few miles from here there is a place where there are big heaps of pots on the bottom. I thought that you were interested in wrecks . . ."

He bent over the table, drawing diagrams in the film of water slopped there by an evening of drinking. I took out my notebook. Prompted by Mustafa, Ahmet Kaptan drew the first of the hundreds of crude diagrams that would someday more than fill the book.

The pots were at a place called Yassi Ada (flat island), fifteen miles from Bodrum. There were hundreds, in two heaps, lying on the bottom in twenty fathoms of water about fifty feet apart. His boat had broken down, but his friend would be glad to take us.

Two days later, in the light of false dawn, we stumbled down to the pier under the castle. The one-lunger in the rickety launch coughed, fired, and we rattled off toward Yassi Ada. The wind rose with the sun. After two hours of smooth going under the lee of the land, we rounded a headland and came out into the channel that separates Kos and Kalymnos from the Turkish mainland. The wind was like a slap in the face. Big swells were beginning to pile up. A group of small islands loomed ahead, some shaped like sugar loaves, others only heaps of rock with seas breaking white over them. The largest looked a little like a sleeping woman with her breasts pointing to the sky. We christened it Marilyn Monroe. Even with a happy sexual connotation, the islands were ugly, fit for shipwrecks and disasters.

Our speed slowed to a laborious crawl as the launch staggered over and into the swells. The boatman squinted at the sun and the hazy sky to the north, and gestured. He said something, a long angry sentence in Turkish. One word was repeated many times: *meltem, meltem.*

Mustafa translated. The wind was getting worse, he said. "We cannot make it today."

I turned on the captain. "No today, no money."

The man turned in silent appeal to Mustafa, who gestured toward a white building on the Turkish shore: "Turgut . . ."

The man flushed, gripped the tiller, and headed us up the channel. Mustafa grinned and explained to me that the building was Turgut's monument. It took me some

time to remember that Turgut had been a great Ottoman admiral under Solyman the Magnificent in the
sixteenth century, when the Ottoman Turks nearly con-
quered Europe. Stranded on the beach, under the hill on
which the monument stood, was the wreck of a big
cargo caïque which, I later learned, had gone ashore in a
bad *meltem* a week or so before. I sympathized with
the boatman, but we could not afford to turn back.

We wiped stinging spray from our faces. It was bitter
cold. We shouted when we saw the flat island that Ahmet Kaptan had described, "one hundred yards long,
shaped like a soup plate," and in an hour were under its
lee. Mustafa looked at the paper with Ahmet's plan,
which seemed very different from our actual surround-
ings.

We ran up to a little cove on the lee side to rest and
smoke. The wind howled. Splashes of spray landed on
us from the waves that were breaking on the weather
side. It was a nasty place, the only vegetation a few
sprouts of weed growing in the crevices of edged rocks
that looked like fangs. The only place where one could
lie or even sit down was a little beach protected from
the wind by a small cliff. I stepped ashore and was
startled by a movement among the driftwood and junk.
A rat scuttled off into a rock crevice. The boatman
gestured at the big seas building up in the channel. His
meaning was clear. If we did not dive and get out pretty
soon, we would stay here all day.

Mustafa allowed that he did not feel up to diving.
Neither did I, but felt obliged, after having bullied the
little boatman. I stripped, and we ran the launch out to
where the wrecks were supposed to lie, twenty fathoms
below the surface of that gray and unfriendly water.

Out of the lee, the wind was stronger. The waves were much too big. The first time we anchored we dragged, as I was struggling to put on my suit. I had thought of the Aegean as a pleasant sea, which shows the extent of my innocence at that time.

My regulator, the device that meters the air from the high-pressure air bottle to the diver, was one of the homemade contraptions I had rented from a doubtful man in Istanbul, who had copied it from a British original. It worked well enough on the surface, but I hesitated, while Mustafa and the boatman looked at me. My real trouble was that I was afraid. I had not been diving for two years. Would my ears clear? Had I forgotten anything? It was cold, and the wind whistled. I saw that Mustafa was as miserable as I, and probably as frightened.

By this time they had gotten the boat back up to the correct place, and anchored again. I held my mask and jumped over. I swam clumsily to the anchor rope and began to go down hand over hand. At ten feet I stopped to make sure that the lung was working well. A little water was coming into the mouthpiece. I swore sourly to myself. The memory of how I once dived for tourists from the glass-bottomed boat, in gear worse than this, seeped back with the realization that the water was clear. The choky sensation of salt water in my throat was familiar.

I looked down. The anchor was just visible, dragging along the bottom in short jerks that threw up clouds of "dust" as waves slapped the boat. If I wanted to go down that reassuring rope I had better hurry. It was moving faster and faster. Now I could clearly see the bottom, which stretched off into eerie blue space behind me and rose, a greenish grass-covered slope, ahead. The anchor rope was almost vertical. I let go, and swam forward and down.

The man had said twenty fathoms, one hundred and twenty feet. I had no depth gauge. On the bottom I hung on to a rocky outcrop and looked around. Was this one hundred and twenty feet? Far above me, the surface was invisible, a faint glimmer of diffused light. It was hard to breathe. I imagined the homemade rubber diaphragm and the delicate adjustments made by the doubtful man, and tried to concentrate. The slope below me stretched out of sight, down into a deep blue nothingness. Ahmet Kaptan had said clearly that the piles of pots lay on a gentle slope. If this was the place, the gentle slope must be below me. I headed down into the deep blue haze that stretched ahead, leaving the light green sea grass behind me.

No, no, not that way, too deep. I shouldn't be this woozy at a hundred and twenty feet. Must be deeper, that's it, must be too deep, swim, swim, up, go up. It's enough, it's the wrong place . . .

I swam slowly up the slope, hardly thinking of what I had come for. I knew that I had to remember to go up, and that I had better go up before that homemade gadget killed me. I glanced around and my eye caught a form. I swam down to look. It was the neck of an amphora sticking up out of the sand. I pulled it, but it would not move. Panting, I rested for a minute, looked around, and saw another, this time just the neck.

I forgot all about the leaky lung and began to follow the trail of broken sherds . . . necks, bottoms, all the same shape. The diver was right. I picked up the broken neck, discarded it, and picked up another. As I swam up the slope, I began to pass rock outcroppings, each one encrusted with pieces of amphoras and indeterminate broken pottery. I tried to pull them loose, but they would not come. I passed a rock with a whole amphora grown solidly to it, the pointed foot at the bottom, the amphora's mouth on the top, and a layer of broken sherds in between, as if the jar had broken on impact when dropped from above, and all the pieces had been frozen together as it broke. I pried at the bottom, thinking that I must get a bottom as well as a top, and must remember the shape. It refused to come loose. I gave up and swam up past the last of the long line of broken amphoras.

I looked up and saw, perhaps eighty feet above me, the waves breaking over the ugly reef, then turned right and swam back across the line of amphoras, hoping that I'd find one of the mounds the diver had seen. There was nothing, just the slope easing off into that blue void on my right, the mud and rock under me, and the line of weed on my left. I began to notice that the air I was breathing was full of salt water. I fought the growing nausea from too much swallowed water, determined to find the wreck. The water won.

As I swam slowly up, fighting the choking, fighting to remember to breathe out and go slow, I glimpsed a mound, possibly of amphoras, off in the direction I had been headed when the lung flooded. I was half drowned and choking, and dared not stop to investigate. I floated in a world of whirling plankton, looked up, and saw the surface gleaming like a mirror over my head. I broke water a hundred yards from the roar of the reef, startled at the crash of breakers and the whine of the wind, after twenty minutes of silence.

The launch stood over to me with a rush and Mustafa, furious, hauled me into the boat. He thought that I had been drowned. They had tried to follow my bubbles, lost them in the waves, and had been half crazy with worry for the last fifteen minutes.

That night we saw Ahmet Kaptan, and I showed him, somewhat accusingly, my hard-won souvenir. He squinted at the sea growth on it and identified it as having come from deep water to the west of the heaps of amphoras. Our mistake seemed simple in retrospect. I was convinced that he was telling the truth. There *were* wrecks at Yassi Ada, lying under the mud I had seen in the lee of that flat, ugly little island.

II

~~~~~

Captain Kemal

The inhabitants will be found captious, rude and un-
civilized, but they are brave and frank, and when their
suspicions and bigotry are not excited, hospitable and
generous. In all intercourse with the shore, therefore,
caution and forebearance are especially requested. Though
each boat should be well provided with arms, they
should be kept out of sight, and every appearance of dis-
trust sedulously avoided . . .

> Captain Beaufort, R.N.
> From his guide to the charts
> made on his Survey of 1812

LATER THAT evening Mustafa and I sat in the cafe, full
of food and raki, trying to raise enough energy to
go back to our lumpy hotel beds. I noticed Mustafa
prick up his ears at a monologue going on at the next
table.

The speaker was obviously drunk. He looked tough.
A battered cloth cap hung over one ear, threatening to
fall off as he pounded the table. He slurred his words. I
looked at him curiously. The eyes, almost hidden under
heavy brows, flicked up and caught mine. They were
black, beady, and without expression. He got up and
came toward me.

The proprietor rushed over and put out a restraining

hand. It was brushed off. I stood up and looked the creature in the eye with the bravest, frankest look that I could muster, and shoved out my right hand. He stopped and took it. We stood for a long breath, squeezing hands and looking into each other's eyes. I said, "Good evening," which just about exhausted my Turkish.

He said, "Good evening," and invited us all to sit down and have a drink. He turned out to be a sponge-boat owner and captain. His name was Kemal. We talked diving until very late. Sometime after midnight he tired of telling us stories about diving and wrecks, and decided he wanted to sing. We sang. It was easy to follow the melody, as these were Turkish folk songs, the kind called *sark*, that sound like funeral dirges in hell. The captain and I sang a very successful number. I imagined I was being impaled and groaned tunefully while he sang the sad, sad words. Everybody cried.

I'll never know how I got to bed. I was wakened by a swarm of flies breakfasting on my scummy eyelids. I remembered a long conversation with the captain in Turkish, a language I did not know I spoke.

While Mustafa and I were drinking our tea, he told me what Captain Kemal had been saying to his friend just before we were formally introduced. "Aqualungs are playthings for tourists, and good Turks should keep the damned pig-eating *giaourlar* [infidels] out of Bodrum, and furthermore . . ."

Our new friend turned up at the hotel at eight o'clock. Although we had forgotten, he remembered that he had invited us to have a look at his boat. We were rowed out in the dinghy by an old man with a secret smile, called Kiasim. Like his captain, he wore a soft cloth cap and a battered business suit. He was Captain Kemal's mate and man-of-all-work. We were to become friends in the years to come.

Mandalinche was the first sponge boat that I had ever been aboard. Thirty-six feet long, she was double-ended and sloop-rigged. The hull was lovely, rather like the famous "Colin Archer" Norwegian fishing boats, but not so deep in the water. The type is called *trechenderi* in Greece, *tirandel* in Turkey. Kemal's boat was an *aktarma*, a variation of the design which had been developed in Kalymnos, the center of sponge diving in Greece, just across the channel from the Bodrum peninsula. An *aktarma* is very maneuverable, a quality necessary to a boat which never anchors while working, and which must keep up with the diver's movements on the bottom.

Most of the deck space was taken up by an open hatch, filled by an old Siebe Gorman German diving compressor. The bottom of the hold was filled with beach-pebble ballast. Lashed to the mast was a Roman amphora which served as the ship's water tank, its tapered bottom jammed into the gravel. I asked Captain Kemal where it had come from.

"We just pull them up from the bottom," he said. "They last longer than new ones."

The crew's quarters, called the *rancha* by Kiasim, had just enough room for the three bunks that slept Kiasim, Captain Kemal, and the top diver. One moved about on hands and knees in a tangle of gear, and slipped sideways into bed. (I was to find out that it was a *rancha* indeed: the crevices of *Mandalinche*'s fo'c'sle were home range to the biggest and meanest fleas in Turkey.) The rest of the crew slept on deck; it was hard to see where they found room. The starboard side was completely taken up by several hundred feet of diving hose, coiled neatly with the helmet in the middle.

The glass ports of the helmet were held in place by what seemed to be ordinary putty, and the grillwork that should protect the glass had been removed. In action, it leaked a continual stream of small bubbles from places where it had been broken and badly soldered. I found out, a long time later, that that helmet had come from Kalymnos in the 1920's. Divers had died in it. The diving suit, which was hung up to dry on the forestay, was ragged and full of patches. Red rubber showed in the places where the outer canvas was worn away.

Abaft the hose and helmet was the fuel tank, an oil drum with a copper pipe leading from its bottom to the engine. Behind it was the "galley," half an oil drum set upright with a layer of sand in the bottom. Brushwood, fuel for this stove, was piled four feet high over the fuel tank. The port side was taken up by two more fifty-gallon oil drums, extra fuel for the engine. They were marked with a swastika and KRIEGSMARINE, and had washed ashore near Captain Kemal's farm in 1943. The ship's standing rigging was improvised from what appeared to have been telephone-pole stays. The boat had not been painted for a long time, but was clean and neat.

Mandalinche's normal complement was six for shallow-water work, and up to fourteen for deep diving. I could not imagine what life would be like aboard that cluttered boat with six on board, let alone fourteen.

Our air bottles were empty and there was no air compressor nearer than Izmir, but Captain Kemal seemed worth talking to. We delayed our departure for Izmir in order to accept his invitation to dine that evening at the *gasinosu*, the "casino."

The kitchen was a mud shack furnished with a trough full of charcoal on which the day's menu simmered in blackened pots. The corpse of a thin goat hung beside the door, covered with sleepy flies, ready to be converted into tough shish kebab by the proprietor, a villainous little man in a dirty apron made from blue mattress ticking. The dining room was a battered arbor set right on the garbage-strewn beach. Its posts were supported on broken classical column drums. Painted on the flaking whitewash of the kitchen shack in large black letters was *Gas IN osU*.

Two or three scrawny mongrel dogs slunk in the shadows outside the pool of light thrown by a pressure lantern hung from a pole of the arbor, under which Captain Kemal was seated at a table with his mate, Kiasim. Already halfway through a liter of raki, they were picking at a plate of watermelon.

They pulled another table up to theirs and shouted for the proprietor. Pitchers of cold water, plates of shish kebab, roast peppers, tomatoes sliced in four parts, beans cooked in red sauce, meatballs, and melons arrived in a rush, accompanied by roars from the kitchen and wails when the boss kicked the cook boy.

Mustafa raised his glass, saying "Merhaba" (greetings), the toast with which the Bodrum men always begin drinking. He began talking, chattering Izmir gossip to the captain and the old man. I sipped my raki and had my first good look at Captain Mustafa Kemal Aras, who became my friend, and whose knowledge was to change the lives of people whom neither he nor I had ever heard of that night.

There was nothing about Kemal that would mark him in a crowd. He was wearing a double-breasted blue suit and a cloth cap which he preferred to the flashy braid-trimmed nautical cap worn by so many Turkish "Kaptans." In the years I knew him, he removed that cap only once for a man, the military governor of the district. He was not tanned, but his face was reddened and roughened from the sun. When he pushed the cap back, his forehead was very white. A toothbrush mustache made his face seem indecisive at first. But when he got up he was curiously quick on his feet. When he poured raki into my glass, I noticed the broadness of his hands in relation to their size, and his deftness with them.

When he spoke, he fixed you with his eyes. You listened. He was very gentle, but when later I sailed with him I saw what I only sensed now, a savage quality of command. The most curious thing about him, which I felt very strongly that evening, was a quality of intellectual curiosity and wonder.

He and his cousin were the last descendants of the Mustafa Pasha who lies in the whitewashed tomb at the harbor entrance opposite the castle. Mustafa Pasha and his son, Djafer, were both grand admirals of the Ottoman navy in the eighteenth century, and the Aras family was almost the last in the district to keep the Ottoman title of *Bey* — sir. When divers from the outer villages addressed Kemal, they called him *Bey* with an air that changed the meaning of the word into something far from the modern usage, where *Bey* means only Mister.

The captain's father had been one of the richest merchants in Bodrum. Kemal, his middle son, was too independent and adventurous to resign himself to life behind a desk. He ran away from home at fourteen to go to sea in sponge boats. When we met him, he had been in the business for twenty-two years, in every kind of diving boat, everywhere up and down the coast from Gallipoli to Iskenderun.

Kemal and Kiasim learned to dive together in a *fernez* boat. Kemal once showed us an old *fernez*. One of the earliest shallow-water diving devices, it was a converted gas mask with double goggles guaranteed to make you cross-eyed under water. Air from a hose went into a breathing bag under the diver's arm and hence to the mask. There was no control of air volume; the diver had to suck what he needed out of the jetstream that whistled by his mouth. They dived naked, holding on to a stone which could be dropped in order to free escape when the device malfunctioned, which it frequently did. In the early days they went to thirty fathoms in these deathtraps. Six divers were killed on the coast the year that the *fernez* was introduced.

After surviving some years on a *fernez* boat, Kemal shipped on a *manjura* or deep diving boat. *Manjuras* are perfectly ordinary boats, except that they specialize in short dives to great depths, using the conventional copper helmet diving gear. A *manjura's* technique is to drag a grapnel in deep water until it hits a rock, say forty fathoms down. The diver is sent down the grapnel line. Kemal said that out of the hundred-odd men that he had seen killed diving, eighty or so were killed on *manjuras*.

Kemal soon became a top *manjura* diver. When the Second World War put a stop to sponge diving on the coast, he went to work as a salvage diver in Istanbul. In 1945 he was given command of the *Mandalinche*, a Kalymnos boat that had carried refugees from the Germans into Myndus (Gumushluk), and had then been purchased and fitted out as a speculative venture by the

local deputy to the National Assembly, a man named
Zeyat Mandalinche. After two years Kemal bought him
out, and become owner of his own ship.

Now he was the most successful sponge captain in
Bodrum. His father had gone broke and died. His brothers were all minor officials with no future. With the proceeds of diving, he had bought some good orange orchards, and was on his way to becoming a prosperous
man.

We did not discover this about Kemal for a long time.
We had decided to stay for another night of talk because
there was something about him that commanded attention: the sharp, vibrant gestures made when he was telling a story, the air of absolute respect with which his
orders were obeyed. As the raki bill went up, the talk
got more and more friendly, but not maudlin as it had
been the night before. Finally, Mustafa decided to tell his
favorite story, the saga of Achi Mehmet:

Once upon a time there was a cook named Achi (cook)
Mehmet who kept an eating house near a caravanserai. Some
say that the serai was on the great road that goes south from
Izmir. Others say that it was in Mugla.

A camel driver came by one day, carrying a load of olive
oil. Achi Mehmet stopped him and asked to have a taste.
Now, if you want to remove a cowskin full of oil from a
camel saddle, you need help. One man holds the off skin,
while the other removes the near one and stows it upright,
leaving you on the empty side with your arms stretched out
over the camel's back, holding the off skin. If you let go, the
oil will fall and a lot of it will spill before you can get around
the camel and set it upright.

"Hang on, friend," said Mehmet. The cameleer obediently
held the one skin while Mehmet removed the other. Then,

judging that the camel man would submit to an outrage to his person rather than lose all the oil in the skin he was holding, Mehmet raped him and walked off with a skin full of oil, whistling.

Camel drivers have mistrusted cooks ever since. If you ask a camel driver if he has seen Achi Mehmet, you are supposed to get a wonderfully violent reaction.

Someone broke in to tell how once a friend of his, driving an old truck between Izmir and Milas, passed a big camel caravan. Feeling playful, he leaned out of his cab and yelled, "Hey, men, have you seen Achi Mehmet?" and drove on in a shower of stones, laughing.

A hundred yards farther on, he had a flat tire. He looked around for a hiding place. There was none. The camel men were coming at a run, waving cudgels. He remembered that there was a burlap sack in the truck, pulled it out, laid it flat on the ground beside the road, and began to pray, knowing that no matter what the provocation, a man praying was not likely to be touched. It took six hours before the camel men left.

The villagers roared with laughter. An extra liter of raki appeared on the table. Kemal slapped Mustafa on the back. He winced, unnoticed in the general amusement. It was the first time that I had heard laughter in the three days that we had been there. Mustafa shouted for silence, drained his glass, and swung into the sequel.

After the olive oil incident, Achi Mehmet became enamored of the beautiful wife of a man from Central Anatolia who was staying at the caravanserai. He made friends with the man, and invited him to his house for food and raki. When the man was very, very drunk, Achi Mehmet said to him that it was now time to go to bed, and as it was late and the serai lay a little far off, he would be welcome to stay. The guest was led to the bedchamber, where he found what appeared to be Achi Mehmet's wife waiting in the bed for him. (It was really a young male friend dressed as a girl.) The man, being a good Moslem, naturally refused to sleep with another man's wife. Achi Mehmet insisted, saying that it was a custom of the district for good friends to offer their wives on occasions like this, that he would be mortally insulted, etc., etc.

The man consented reluctantly, drew his big sword, put it on the bed between the "wife" and himself, and slept.

A few days later, the man asked Mehmet to his house. They drank a lot, and in the end the man was obliged to offer Mehmet the hospitality of the house, including his wife. In defense of the host, it must be said that Achi Mehmet had told him that the custom was a very old one, and of course no honorable man would take advantage of it.

Mehmet was led to the bridal chamber, where he enjoyed himself immensely while the unfortunate lady's husband slept. The next morning the husband woke to find his wife weeping bitterly.

"Why, oh why, dear husband, did you let that man do such things to me?"

The man was furious. Bursting with rage, he saddled his big horse, oiled and loaded his big blunderbuss, made sure that his sword was free in its sheath and his pistols loose in his sash, and went looking for Mehmet. It was early in the morning, when camel drivers like to travel. There were many on the road. Each time the man passed one, he asked, "Have you seen Achi Mehmet?"

It brought down the house. Kemal guffawed. Kiasim, who had been meditatively peeling a hot pepper, nearly fell off his chair, choked, and had to be revived with a big gulp of raki.

Mustafa and I had to tell the story again and again as new friends arrived in the cafe. It was marvelously effective if I gave the punch line, "Have you seen Achi Mehmet?" (It was the first Turkish phrase I learned after "good morning" and "good night.") Our social success was assured.

All that year people whom I had never seen before would approach me on the street and whisper "Achi Mehmet," until I got sick of it and lost my temper one night with a stranger who was openly calling *me* Achi Mehmet. Of all Mustafa's public relations gimmicks and improvisations of the next years, Achi Mehmet was the most successful.

The rest of the evening was brilliant. We argued about everything under the sun. The captain told wonderful stories which Mustafa had no time to translate. I nearly went mad with frustration as the captain and Kiasim told of wrecks, fights, treasures, mountains of amphoras, smuggling, village scandal, and politics. The upshot of it all was that we were invited to spend a few weeks on their boat. They promised that if we were looking for junk under the sea they would guide us to acres of it.

We staggered off to bed, leaving them singing sad songs and talking about the good old days. Next morning, feeling awful, we crawled onto the bus for the miserable trip to Izmir. We had made a start in Bodrum.

III

~~~~~

The Innocent Adventurers

THE TALES Mustafa and I had heard seemed so promising that I was determined to go on. Our inquiries about the bronze Demeter had been inconclusive, but it did not matter. There were many other wrecks.

I knew that, with one exception, no sponge divers had ever voluntarily shown things to outsiders. The exception had been spectacular. In 1901, a captain from Symi named Demetrios Kondos found the wreck of a ship loaded with statues, probably looted about 80 B.C., during the Roman occupation of Greece. Antikythera, where Kondos had found his famous wreck, was over two hundred miles from the Carian coast. Still, the discovery of the Demeter might mean that the same kind of thing existed here.

Captain Kondos had reported his discovery. Other discoverers had not. Another treasure ship was found by Greek sponge divers at Mahdia, in the Bay of Tunis, in 1907. They tried to sell the bronzes they found, but were discovered by the alert director of the Department of Antiquities in Tunis, who made them tell him the location. An American philanthropist put up the money

to raise some of the material, and the art works found
fill several galleries in the Bardo museum.

In 1926 some Greek trawlermen found a bronze statue
off Cape Artemision and tried to sell it. They too were
noticed by alert authorities. The bronze, which was
nearly broken up by the fishermen when they got into
trouble, stands in the Athens museum today. One of the
finest surviving fifth-century bronzes, it is a larger-than-
life statue of Poseidon.

One of the glories of the Louvre is a fifth-century
B.C. bronze Apollo brought up by a trawler from the
channel between Piombino and Elba in 1832. The exact
location is now forgotten.

In 1840 a German traveler passing through Skiathos
heard that the year before a bronze statue had come up
in a trawl and had been sold to an Englishman. In 1901 a
hoard of copper ingots of the middle Bronze Age was
salvaged off Euboea by sponge divers working on the
Kyme breakwater. They were nearly sold for scrap, but
were accidentally noticed by an archaeologist and are
now safely in the Athens museum. In June of 1925
trawlermen dragged up a life-size fourth-century
bronze in the Bay of Marathon. A bronze lamp base
and some rotten wood came up in the same haul of the
net, good evidence that the trawl had caught on a shipwreck, sunk almost below the surface of the mud.

The list of spectacular finds from the sea goes on and
on. Less spectacular discoveries are seldom reported.
Every Aegean fishing village has its collection of ancient
amphoras found by net fishermen. Often they are so
common that they are built into houses as decorations.

By the time that I arrived in Bodrum in 1958, there
had been a long series of underwater "excavations."

Most had been stigmatized by accidents. All were characterized by confusion of purpose. The salvagers had found wood, sheathing, and unidentified bits of ship material, but no one had ever published an accurate drawing made under water. Even photographs of a hull in place were rare. Archaeologists on land perform technical miracles of the highest order. The Viking ship found at Sutton Hoo in England in the 1930's was excavated so carefully that detailed plans of the hull of the ship could be made, although the wood had completely perished. I wondered why, when confronted with actual wood in good condition, the sea diggers up to the present had not even produced sketch plans or accurate measurements.

The answer lay, perhaps, in the nature of the underwater medium. Anyone who dived automatically became an "expert." The archaeologists understood very little about working underwater and left the actual labor to the "experts," who committed archaeological atrocities right and left. Divers tend to be adventurous types, not given to sympathy with the archaeologists' interest in broken pots.

If, as I now suspected, the Turkish Aegean were a treasure house of ancient wrecks, and we should be able to record them, it might someday, somehow, be possible to get the money and equipment and personnel necessary to do an underwater job that would prove to the world that underwater archaeology was a practical proposition, and to convince people that ships and their cargoes could be as interesting as inscriptions and statues.

One of Mustafa Kapkin's best friends in Izmir was director of the museum there. We spent an evening with him, talking about the possibilities of underwater archaeology. Hakki Gultekin was a dedicated and idealistic archaeologist who agreed that it was important to find out what we could while we had the chance. I am sure that he was not convinced that the hull of a ship could be preserved in mud after thousands of years. However, the evidence that *something* was there stood in his museum, in the form of the fourth-century bronze bust that had come from Bodrum.

Our project worked itself out over the table in Mustafa's garden. Mustafa and I would go back to Bodrum. We would try to find out all we could about the ancient wrecks known to the sponge divers. Hakki Bey, as museum director, would take charge of the project, under the auspices of the Izmir Museum.

In Mustafa I had an invaluable partner and ally. At thirty-seven he was one of the best photographers in Turkey, and the first Turk to make underwater photographs. His Cretan background had given him a love for the sea and an affection for the coast people, which they respected.

Both Mustafa and I believed that Captain Kemal could take us to wreck sites. But it was impossible to accompany him and dive unless we had a high-pressure air compressor for filling aqualung bottles, and decent equipment was unobtainable in Turkey for any price. Hakki Bey, Mustafa, and I shook hands on our project, and next morning I started off on my search for gear via the biweekly plane from Izmir to Athens.

Athens was pleasant, after months in Asia, but lacking in air compressors of the type I needed. It was there I met the person whose advice and moral support made the whole project possible. Someone in Izmir had suggested that I see a lady in Athens who knew all about amphoras. I wrote her and received an invitation to visit her in her office at the Stoa of Attalos in the Athenian agora. Miss Virginia Grace made me feel at home, gave me tea, and patiently made sense of my confused ideas of what I hoped to do in Turkey. I got on the boat for Italy with new confidence in what I was attempting.

For a while it seemed that it was going to be impossible to find the right kind of compressors in Italy, but at last I found Franco Ingegnoli in Milan. He managed a diving shop, and had what was probably the only portable air compressor in Italy. This he let me have on credit, and a plastic underwater camera case as well.

Two weeks later I arrived in Izmir with the compressor, one wet suit, two regulators, and one set of double tanks, after a hysterical three-day session with the Istanbul customs. They decided to let the madman and his strange gear through only after I lost my temper and began dragging the box containing my gear to the side of the dock, meaning to drop it over the edge and leave Turkey by the next plane.

In June of 1958, armed with our pitiful equipment, very little money, and the conviction that we were going to find something wonderful, Mustafa Kapkin and I boarded the country bus for Bodrum and our promised place on *Mandalinche*. When we arrived, she was at sea. No one knew when she would return. We rented a big room on the ground floor of the hotel, explored the castle and the town, and began to make friends with the villagers.

Bodrum was beautiful that spring. The hills were still green, and in the early morning ringneck doves cooed on every rooftop in the village. In the hot afternoons I used to climb into the ruined castle and spend the heat of the day dozing with a book, or swim off the breakwater.

Finally Kemal arrived. He was glad to see us. After some days of delay we got our equipment aboard *Mandalinche* one evening and went to bed very early. Kemal, as he had promised, would show us those piles of pots in the sea near Yassi Ada.

IV

~~~~~

Our First Wreck

WE WERE wakened at 3 A.M. by Kiasim, were off by four, and at dawn had reached a village at the end of the peninsula. We went alongside a modern concrete dock and tied up to a bollard made from an ancient altar, with bulls' heads on its side and an unintelligible Greek inscription.

We drank tea in a pleasant cafe with an arbor of vines over it supported by ancient columns, and a few hours later were rolling in the slight swell off Yassi Ada, the flat island of the month before. At an order from Captain Kemal, Kiasim turned the tiller over to another diver, clambered over the cluttered deck to the dressing bench, and began pulling on the ragged diving dress. The ship's boy rushed to tighten the wing nuts that held the canvas to the heavy breastplate. Captain Kemal rigged the twenty-pound lead weights, running the traditional lashings into the soft cotton rope with flicks of his square hands. The old man bowed his head. Kemal picked up the helmet and slipped it carefully over his ears, holding it so the bronze threads would meet properly, and twisted until they locked.

The boy jumped to slip the compressor's drive belt over the engine flywheel. Kiasim hung one foot over the side and hunched, waiting for the signal. Kemal stood in the bows, making hand signals to the man at the tiller, who eased the boat up to the ugly green stain that marked the reef. Kemal tapped the helmet and Kiasim dropped overboard with a splash, to float for ten seconds before sinking with a sigh of escaping air.

I put on mask, fins, and snorkel, and jumped in after him. Twenty feet below, he was walking over the rocky bottom, crouching almost on his knees as he pulled the hose behind him. He stopped every few seconds to feel for sponges under rocks. Air bubbles burst from the helmet and floated toward me, expanding as they rose. He stopped. I heard Mustafa yelling, only faintly because of the pound of the swell on the seething reef. I looked up.

"It's there, it's there!"

I saw nothing but stones, whitish with black flecks on them, but decided to take Mustafa's word for it. I took five deep breaths and swam down the line to where the diver stood erect, swaying in the swell. Halfway, I realized that he was standing on a heap of potsherds, and that what I had thought were white stones were in reality broken amphoras, scattered over the bottom to beyond my range of vision in the clear water.

I swam to Kiasim, rapped "Shave and a haircut, bay rum," on the copper helmet, and was gratified to see him jump. I peeped into the glass port. The old man grinned. We shook hands and I dashed for the surface, out of air. He told me afterwards that it was the first time in nearly forty years of diving that he had seen another diver underwater.

I rushed to strap on my aqualung. By the time I was ready, we were over blue water away from the reef and it was time for Kiasim to surface. I waited, sweating in the foam rubber suit, while they dressed a second diver.

The rest of that day passed in frantic attempts at photography, largely frustrated because our cameras were not working well, and arguments with Captain Kemal and Mustafa, who were bored by my interest in amphoras.

We did not find the deep wrecks on beds of mud that Ahmet Kaptan had told us about. Instead, we found others, not wrecks in the accepted sense of the word but masses of broken pottery scattered on the reef. They had to be wrecks. How else could one explain a thousand identical amphoras on an isolated reef a long way from land?

On our way back to Bodrum we stopped to fish at a reef that lay just off the cape that turns from the channel into Bodrum bay and found, instead of fish, masses of broken pottery, bits of metal, and a heap of building stones. The Kos channel was a remarkable marine graveyard. There was work here for all summer and years to come.

Back in Bodrum, we decided to move to the islands for a week, build a camp, and explore systematically. Mustafa had personal business to settle in Izmir. He suggested that we go back to Izmir, call a meeting of the interested members of the Izmir Diving Club, and return to Yassi Ada with them.

In Izmir we had dinner with Hakki Bey, our patron and sponsor. He told us that a villager had turned up from Bodrum with a wild story about the valuable antiquities that foreigners were stealing from the sea.

Hakki Bey had reassured him. The man was apparently referring to the half-dozen amphora necks from Yassi Ada that were now stored on the roof of the little Bodrum hotel.

Hakki Bey had hopes of raising money in Ankara, which could be given to the diving club for our project, but was worried about the attitude of some of the classical archaeologists to whom he had spoken. They believed that our project was a fantasy, and that amateurs intruding upon their professional world should be discouraged. A rumor which interested me greatly was that the King of Sweden had asked permission to investigate the Demeter find several years before, and had been refused.

That night I wrote in my diary: "We are fantastically lucky that the powers that be have not stopped us from carrying through this project. I cannot believe that all is smooth politically . . ."

I mentioned this to Hakki Bey the next time I visited him in his office at the museum. He sent out for a cup of tea, and told me the old story of the man who was told that death would come to him on a certain day. He understood the prophesy to mean that death would come to his village, so he took a special trip to Damascus.

There, in the court of the great mosque, he was greeted by a stranger who approached, asked his name, and said, "I did not expect to meet you in Damascus, on this day."

"What is written, is written," said the little museum director. "What will come is in the hands of God. Meanwhile, there is no law which says that you cannot go swimming in the sea."

We drained our tea and went to look at the bronze in

her glass case. She is a sad, beautiful prototype of a Renaissance virgin, with the scars of the dragger's wire on her neck above the frill of her shift, just visible above the beautifully draped robe. Demeter. I burned to know where she had come from. What ship carried her? From where? To where? Was she part of a cargo like the Poseidon of Artemision or the Philosopher of Antikythera? No one knew. The answer to the question and to many others lay in deep water off Bodrum.

Mustafa found a battered station wagon for hire and, two days later, we loaded our mountains of gear into it together with the divers Mustafa had persuaded to join us. We had a good crew. Ilhan, reputedly the best spear fisherman in Turkey, was burly, barrel-chested, and engagingly ugly. He had started the first factory for the manufacture of spear guns in Turkey that year, and was accompanied by a bundle of lethal-looking new weapons for testing.

Mustafa's best friend, Rasim, introduced himself in good German and immediately began to crack jokes about broken amphoras. A refugee from the Crimea, he was an engineer in a factory in Izmir, and had designed and built the compressed air lungs which he and Mustafa were using. Erhan, the third member of the group, was an electrical engineer who worked with Rasim, a quiet and steady little man.

We talked loudly, sometimes shouting to make ourselves heard over the rattle of the rotten car on the bumpy road. When talk died, we stopped and drank tea in a place where Mustafa, as usual, seemed to know everyone.

The road led past Ephesus, where St. Paul preached,

and into an area of twisting road and pine forest. We had a flat tire on a curve in the road between two great boulders big as houses, with thyme all around, its fragrance crisp in the brassy sunlight. Rasim looked around while the driver cursed and banged at the tire, and remarked that *zeybeks*, bandits, had haunted this road in the 1920's. The clatter of arms was gone, and the sound of shepherds' pipes flowed down the mountain.

A file of village women in red skirts rounded the curve in the road. Barefoot, slim-legged, carrying their shoes in their hands, they were bent double with great bundles of grass. As we were heaving on the car to raise it so that the repaired tire could be put on (naturally the jack was broken), others came by with a herd of goats. A big billy coughed and grunted as a girl, her face carefully concealed in a striped shawl, wheedled it past the car. At the end of the procession swaggered an old woman, whistling like a boy. She called harshly to the animals and strode past us, straight-backed like a drillmaster with recruits, looking neither to the right nor to the left.

I dozed as the darkness overtook us and we crept up into the last chain of mountains. I awoke to the jolt of the car stopping in a mountain clearing where Mustafa and I had drunk tea the week before. Cool mountain water poured endlessly into an overflowing tank. The old man came out and gave us his greeting — "Merhaba" — and took my hand. I was pleased to be recognized by this nameless old man in his clearing on the mountain.

His son brought us hard-boiled eggs mixed with thin yogurt, followed by fried eggs. Mustafa asked him for raki.

"I'll have to ask Daddy," he answered in a small voice. We drank tea. The old man crooned a half-remembered song, accompanying himself with a three-stringed mandolin that he tweaked into strange but pleasing minor trills. The crickets sang.

It was very late when we got to Bodrum. We pounded on the hotel door, got no answer, and stretched out on the concrete porch, to be wakened by the inevitable flies.

The hotelkeeper was furious because we had wakened him the night before. No vacancies, he said. After protests from Mustafa and the others, he gave us a big room on the ground floor. Mustafa remarked later that the man was just too lazy to get up and show us the place. It was simpler to say "No vacancies."

Captain Kemal came to visit us and admire Mustafa's new underwater movie camera case and other equipment. We spent the day tinkering with our diving gear. A succession of characters turned up to drink tea and tell interminable diving stories.

One gaffer offered to show us an underwater cave, accessible only to a free diver because its twistings and turnings would foul a helmet diver's hose. "The Venetians hid their treasures there when *they* left," he said, eying me sidewise. "The treasure hunter who does not know the spell will be burned with a terrible itching and *die* when he finds the gold."

He offered to show us the place, and split with us fifty-fifty. Generous of him, we thought. Another old man knew of a treasure around the point near Bodrum. The army maintained a post nearby. Why else but to guard the treasure?

They were obsessed by the idea of gold in the sea and under the earth, and believed that the ancients had buried quantities of it in the most unlikely places. One sees pits dug by treasure hunters near every ancient site in Turkey. With one exception, we never met anybody who had found gold, in all the years we worked in Bodrum. But there was always someone who knew someone, in the next village or the village after, who had found something, perhaps a gold ring, perhaps a bit of pathetic jewelry from a Hellenistic tomb, worth little but exaggerated, as the tale drifted through the impoverished villages, into enough shining gold to burden a donkey.

That night we dined with Kemal and his crew in the sad *gasinosu* and heard more stories. One of Kemal's men claimed to have seen a tower in forty fathoms to the base. It rose twenty fathoms, he said, and fish swam in and out of the marble-linteled doorways. Later, when I got to know him well, I discovered that the dimensions of the tower grew in proportion to his intake of raki. One glass raised it about three fathoms. He always got incoherent and had to go home before the imaginary tower actually broke water.

The evening, like most other evenings spent with Captain Kemal and Mustafa, degenerated into untranslatable stories, and I was left silent in a corner. It was decided that we would leave for Yassi Ada the next day.

I woke wondering unhappily why everything in Turkey had to be accompanied by so much raki. If I were to drink like my Turkish friends, I should soon be a wreck. As it was, they drank twice as much as I and were twice as tough. Their staple, yogurt, must preserve them.

The day dragged on in dismal anticipatory tinkering. The captain finally turned up at 5 P.M. to say we could not leave until the next day. Mustafa's friend, Erhan, the electrical engineer, decided to make an underwater

[47]

flash gun. A fiendish gadget, its batteries were in a tube of aluminum, sealed off with road tar. The socket was swiped from a wrecked house next door. The reflector was the bottom of a cheap vase. A weird and wonderful device; I hoped it would not electrocute the user. Fortunately, it didn't work at all.

I wandered around Bodrum, wondering about the broken bits of ancient buildings built into the walls of the modern houses, remnants of the ancient town of Halicarnassus. Its glory had been the Mausoleum, the tomb of Mausolus, greatest of the Carian kings. Built by his widow, Artemesia, that extravagant monument had been one of the seven wonders of the ancient world, and had stood for nearly two millennia until the Knights of St. John had demolished it and used its stone for St. Peter's castle. The modern name, Bodrum, is only a corruption of Petronium.

The town had an aura of the past. Its monuments and public buildings aside, it cannot have appeared very different to Alexander the Great or Cicero, or Herodotus, who was born there. I walked up to the ancient theater, which faced toward the sea so that the audience had a wonderful view of the island of Kos, where modern medicine began, and tried to figure out from the guidebook where the public buildings of the ancient town might have stood.

I found it hard to concentrate, being too worried about whether we were really going to leave the next day, and if Ahmet Kaptan's story of the heaps of pots in the sea in deep water off Yassi Ada were true. I suspected that it might be only drunken babble, mouthed to make the evening pass well, and maintained the morn-

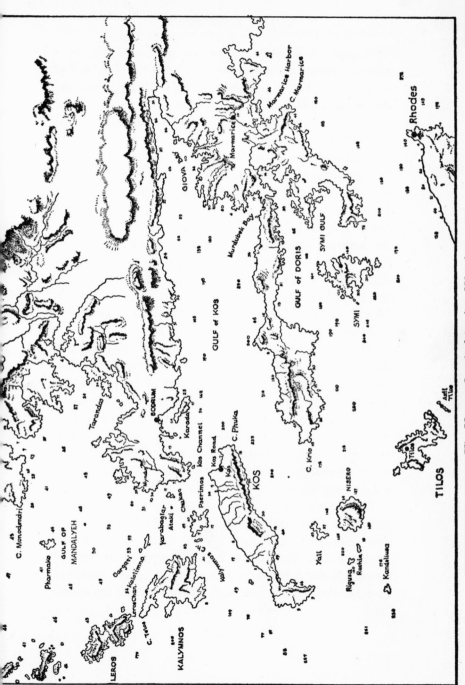

The Harvest Land of Ancient Wrecks

ing after out of simple pride. After lunch that day, Kiasim appeared with a handcart. We loaded all our gear onto *Mandalinche*, and at dawn the next day we set out for Yassi Ada.

V

~~~~~

The Ship Trap

IN THE VILLAGE where the Greeks used to live, with the bull's-head altar bollard on the pier, we bought two camel baskets full of green peppers and sweet, ripe tomatoes with the taste of sun in them, then heaved in the anchor and rounded the cape into the rising wind. We headed for the largest island, where there was a cove with good holding ground for small ships, and a good beach for camping under the cliffs which sheltered both ships and men from the force of the north wind. Standing at the tiller in the bucking boat, with spray running down his cheeks, Kiasim waved to the west.

"Goddam Greeks," he said. He pointed out the islands of Kos, Kalymnos, and Pserimos. "We owned them once."

We were headed for the Chattal group, which forms a no-man's-land between Greece and Turkey. The eight major islands and several reefs and rocks lie on the route that one must take if coasting from north to south or vice versa. In the center of an area in which great historical events have taken place, they play little part in recorded history, and I had learned little about them in the libraries of Athens.

In 1599 Master Thomas Dallan, merchant, three days out of Rhodes, bound for Constantinople in the ship *Hektor* of London, twenty-seven guns, wrote in his diary, "Standing on the spar deck of our ship, I toulde no less than sixteen islands which were round about us . . ."

As we struggled up the channel, I understood Dallan better. *Hektor* must have been standing up Chuka channel, just off Yassi Ada. The sixteen islands were Kalymnos, seven miles to the westward; Kos, six miles south; Pserimos, two and a half miles southwest; Kalolimno to the north, and farther north still, almost lost in the haze, Leros and the tiny island of Pharmako, which stands like a sentry at the entrance to the Gulf of Mandalyeh. These islands, together with the nine islands of the Chattal group, make fifteen. It is probable that (as I did the first time I saw it) the Elizabethan merchant Dallan counted Karabaglar as two islands, for the sandy spit that connects its two parts merges with the sea until one is right upon it. We planned to camp there.

A little to the north of Karabaglar the *Hektor* was shadowed by four ominous rowing galleys which sheered off when the English beat to quarters and then stood out to sea, away from the Turkish mainland.

The Chattal group must have been the training ground for the naked sponge divers of Kalymnos. Beaufort found them working there in 1811. "Some small rocks near the coast produce sponges, which the Greek islanders of Kalymnos are remarkably expert at picking. We had an opportunity of witnessing the operation. The little knob of rock, from which the sponge was to be detached, was forty feet below the surface of the sea. The divers took it in turns to descend, remaining underwater between two and three minutes. When quite exhausted they were drawn up by a rope and laid out on the deck of the boat to recover . . ."

Today the islets belong to Turkey. They are still a good sponge-fishing ground. Draggers work the deep water, Kemal and the other diving captains work the rocks, and the little naked sponge diver galleys stay by the shallow reefs.

We anchored out of the wind in the cove of Karabaglar, which is the biggest of the islands. By the time we were ready to cross the half-mile stretch of sea to Yassi Ada, the wind was too strong, so I climbed the peak of the big island and watched great seas break on the sheer cliffs of the north side. The wind almost blew me away. It was the *meltem*, the savage seasonal northwesterly wind of the Aegean. In summer the Aegean sea is northwestward of the deep and extensive seasonal low-pressure area over Iran and northwestern India. Nature abhors a vacuum, and the cold air of the steppes of northeastern Europe rushes to fill it, making the Aegean seaman miserable by its passage. For three months a year the wind rises in the morning, gradually increasing until it is blowing half a gale by midafternoon, and dropping at evening to flat calm just after dark.

From the big island's peak I could see Yassi Ada, where our wrecks lay. Watching the boil of waves on the west reef, I came to a clearer understanding of why shipwrecks lay there. Yassi Ada was the westernmost of the group. One hundred yards to the west of it was the reef, invisible from sea level, its top just below the surface. A prudent seaman would want to clear the whole Chattal group, thinking, "Why pick your way among those rocks if you don't have to?" He would be running, at this time of year, before the *meltem*, if he were headed from the north toward Rhodes, seventy miles away, or Halicarnassus, fifteen miles away from Yassi Ada. He would want to stay away from the lee shore of Pserimos or Kos, six miles downwind. So he would stay close to Yassi Ada, then sail on a broad reach: twelve miles to go with a lee shore under him all the way until he was free of the easternmost point of Kos and ready to stand away for Rhodes or Knidos or

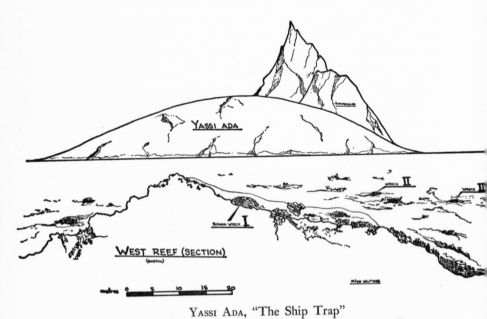

YASSI ADA, "The Ship Trap"

The entire slope, from the shallow place where all the ships struck to the heap of amphoras at the end of the rock at the right edge of the drawing, is covered with broken pottery.

Kos harbor. Not wanting to go too close to the outermost island, and knowing that almost all Aegean islands are steep-to, he would stand a cable length off and, running before the strong *meltem* in fairly heavy seas, would be on the reef before he could do a thing about it. Yassi Ada was, and is, a very subtle ship trap.

In the little bay where *Mandalinche* anchored, gusts of the dying *meltem* bouncing off the cliffs blew ripples across the water in patterns that changed like rubbed velvet. The peaks all around turned from red and gold to gray as the sun fell behind Kalymnos. The little Italian compressor's popping came up to me in waves, distorted by the wind.

My mind full of lost ships waiting to be discovered in the morning, I clambered down, careful not to cut myself on the jagged edges of the volcanic rock, and looking out for scorpions. Kiasim was tending a fire over which simmered a big pot of fish stew. Mustafa was cutting up salad. The compressor blatted, too loud for that peaceful place. I went to help Rasim set up the tent.

We agreed that the first thing to do next day was to search the deep water south of Yassi Ada for the two piles of amphoras that Ahmet Kaptan had told us about. The masses of broken pots on the reef could wait. One of the heaps was said to be at seventeen fathoms, one hundred and two feet. We decided that I would go off the east end of Yassi Ada and follow the seventeen-fathom line with the depth gauge.

Early the next morning I dropped off *Mandalinche*'s diving ladder and swam along the bottom over sand until I came to the weed-grown rock ledge. The depth gauge said thirty feet. The slope loomed below, falling to deep blue-green haze, as terrifying as it had been on the first dive. I swam down slowly, and gasped when I hit a layer of icy water fifty feet down. At sixty feet the bottom was still rocky. I noticed the neck of a broken amphora in a crevice of the rock. I picked it up. It was the same one that I had picked up on my first dive. At eighty feet the ridge still fell at a steep angle with no sign of a leveling off to the sloping mud bottom that Ahmet Kaptan had described so clearly.

The ridge was full of fish. Big groupers watched me quizzically from under rocks, their forefins twiddling like helicopter rotors. One lay in a patch of grass a foot away. I thought it would impress the others if I caught a ten-pound grouper for dinner with only the sponge trident that I had brought along for prying pots off rocks. I came very close. He twiddled himself down into a patch of grass. I stabbed him in the head, and he scuttled away with a strip of white flesh flopping from the top of his head. Another grouper, smaller, lay on top of a big sponge, watching me with sad, accusing eyes. I was ashamed. I had the privilege of being a foot away from a beautiful, friendly, wild thing, and all I could think of was killing it.

I swam along the slope at seventeen fathoms. The slope of broken rock rose above me and to my right. To my left, the steep slope led to nothing. I swam down it and found no leveling-off place. No wreck could have slid down that broken rock surface. At one hundred and thirty feet the slope continued. At one hundred and fifty feet it still continued. At one hundred and seventy-five feet I began to feel dopey and depressed. My air came hard. The dive was over.

I swam upwards, angling across the slope. At sixty feet, I looked up at the rippled surface and saw the reassuring shape of Mustafa's friend, Ilhan, swimming above me. I hung below him to decompress at ten feet. He swam down and made faces at me. When I surfaced, *Mandalinche* was rolling harder, the sea was getting up, and the wind was beginning to whistle in the rigging.

On the second dive I went down the slope to one hundred feet, and followed a steep sand slide along the side of the island, feeling like a fly on a wall. In ten minutes I came to rock again. A line of scattered amphora fragments lay along the slope. Forty feet higher the bottom was covered with them, as far as one could see. Farther up the slope the bottom was a solid field of potsherds, over one hundred feet long by fifty wide. It was the wreck that we had seen on the first day with Kemal and *Mandalinche*. There were thousands of jars, mostly broken, all with similar shapes, hook handles, and pointed bottoms. In Athens months later, Miss Grace identified them as a type manufactured in Rhodes during the first century A.D.

A complete jar lay half covered by broken sherds. I saw the shape of the dinghy above me, surfaced, got a rope from Mustafa, and swam down to free the jar. The conglomerate came loose easily. I jerked three times after tying the rope to the neck. Mustafa pulled it up, but not fast enough. The amphora bumped heavily along the bottom as the dinghy pitched in the swell. The bottom broke off as I watched, horrified. It was a lesson in the fragility of pottery that had lain two thousand years in the sea.

I heaved my empty tanks into the dinghy after the amphora and swam to *Mandalinche*. She was rolling madly, and the wind was now screaming in her rigging. It was impossible to work in the big sea built up by the *meltem*. We ran the narrow channel to the camp on the big island for our lunch, and slept and spearfished all afternoon.

We spent four days exploring the west reef, and every day were driven off before noon by the *meltem*, which began gently at around eight in the morning and turned the flat, beautiful sea into a raging maelstrom over the reef by early afternoon. Every day we tried to work too long, against the buildup of the wind and swell, and every day we learned a new part of the big lesson. The *meltem* was not to be fooled with.

Mandalinche had been hauled out the week before and her stone ballast removed for repairs to her bottom. She rolled so badly that it was difficult to get the jars, laboriously chipped out of the sea growth on the bottom, over the side without breaking them. It was impossible to anchor on the steeply sloping rock, so Kiasim ran her up to the rocks, dropped the divers, and stood behind the shelter of the reef until we surfaced and waved for him. The weather got worse. Every day we were driven back earlier, to swelter angrily on the beach for the rest of the day. The continual bad weather made photography almost impossible, as the water was always dirty over the reef where the wrecks lay.

On the fifth day, working on the outer pile of amphoras, I was startled to see a naked diver. It was Mustafa, frantically signaling me. I surfaced immediately and saw what was wrong. The seas coming over the reef were so bad that *Mandalinche* could not stay there. I waved, and swam over to her. Kiasim, bareheaded because his cap would not stay on against the wind, was alone at the tiller. The little ship was pitching half her length out of water at every big wave. I wondered how he could keep his feet when he ran forward to drop the diving ladder on the starboard side just forward of the shrouds.

He ran the boat carefully up to me. I grabbed the ladder, struggling to hang on and climb up, and was pulled back by the hungry waves and the weight of the double tanks. I wrestled the flapping ladder, kicking desperately against the force of the waves. When I got a foothold I hung, exhausted, with my arms inside the bulwark, my clumsy flippered feet maintaining a weak toehold on the ladder. The air came hard. I choked and spat out the mouthpiece. I had used up the last air in my tanks struggling to get to the boat and hang on.

There was no screen on the bronze screw, which gleamed gold in a smother of foam as the boat pitched her stern clear out of the water. I clung, using all my strength to keep my fingers curved around the inside of the bulwark, unable to move against the sea's drag on my legs, remembering a photograph I had once seen of the horribly mutilated body of a man who had gone into a propeller.

I waited for a roll that would allow me to swing over the bulwark. The compressor swung with a twisting roll of the boat and, as I watched, slid toward me across the deck. I screamed for Kiasim. He could not even hear me in the roar of the wind and the crash of waves on the reef. I glanced at the propeller, gritted my teeth, and clung. The compressor smashed against my wrists, and left one arm hurting like hell and the other with no feeling at all. On the next starboard-side downroll I managed to crawl over the bulwark and lay sobbing, twitching with pain and shock on the wet deck, too weak to do more than curse feebly, thinking, There goes the summer, I've broken my arm.

Kiasim ran *Mandalinche* back under the lee of the island, left her to herself, and came forward to help me out of my gear. I wedged myself into a corner, gritted my teeth, and flexed both hands. They worked. My arm was not broken. We hauled the other men on board and headed home, defeated for the moment by the rise of hot air in India and Iran.

The *meltem*, behind us on the run toward Hussein point and the calm of Bodrum bay, lost its frightening force and became just a good fresh breeze that pushed us faster home. We unloaded our pots onto the dock in Bodrum in the presence of a gathering crowd that stared condescendingly at the crazy American and his piles of useless junk. We were all caked, soaked with salt. I thought of the fountain in front of the mosque, just across the dock from where *Mandalinche* was tied, looked around the cluttered deck for a bucket, and found none. My eye lit upon a clay cooking pot, one of those salvaged from the west reef.

As I dipped water with it I thought, "No one has used this pot for two thousand years." I picked it up carelessly next morning, and it broke of its own weight.

We had learned a lot that week. It was clear now that the Yassi Ada reef was the last resting place of many ships. The largest of them must have been the ship that carried the pointed jars with the hooked handles which lay piled on the crest of the reef. From their position, I had a clear impression of how the ship must have gone onto the reef, swung broadside, and broken into two pieces, scattering thousands of amphoras down the slope.

We had found dozens of different kinds of cooking pots, pieces of copper, and bits of wood preserved in the sand.

We knew now that complete jars had to be filled with water and dried slowly in the shade to prevent their cracking. My trip to Italy for equipment had not been a waste of time and money. There was more at Yassi Ada than I had ever dreamed of. I itched for the day that we would find the deep wrecks and explore the rest of the west reef.

VI

∞∞∞∞∞

Devil

MY LETTER in his hand, the postal clerk studied the catalogue, squinting doubtfully at the yellowed pages.

"Morocco yok," * said he.

"*Is* Morocco," I replied.

I struggled to remember the Turkish for "map." If I could show him Morocco on a map, he might admit its existence. The little police spy who followed me everywhere in Bodrum sat, indifferent, in the corner. Finally the clerk, exhausted by the effort, suggested that we telephone the director, who was at home having a siesta. The telephone, naturally, didn't work. He suggested a cup of tea. The idea of a place so far away that a postal clerk had never heard of it pleased me.

We had not finished our tea when a small, breathless boy burst in to announce that two "Americans" had arrived and were looking for me. I left my "shadow" and the postmaster discussing the whereabouts of Morocco, and found the visitors in the cafe. They were English and, to my indescribable joy, were also draftsmen. John

* *Yok:* no.

Carswell taught art at the American University of Beirut, and had drawn pots for archaeologists all over the Middle East. Honor Frost had worked for one of the most thorough of modern archaeologists, Miss Kathleen Kenyon, at Jericho in Palestine. Furthermore, she was a handsome blonde.

As conversation continued, she remarked, "I've brought my valve and bottle."

I replied that that was nice, and that raki did in fact get a bit tiresome, then did a double take and realized that she meant aqualung and tank. She was a diver, having learned in the south of France after World War II at about the time I had worked for old Charley in Honolulu.

She had been absorbed with the idea of developing workable underwater drafting techniques ever since she had worked for Miss Kenyon, and had come to Turkey in the hope of finding an ancient shipwreck on which to experiment. She was provided with a small British aqualung, an alcohol stove, a thick notebook, a red bathing suit, a packet of China tea, and a lot of luck, for she had gone to see Rasim's factory in Izmir and had there succeeded in getting her bottle filled. Fatih Bekbey at the factory had told her about the "mad American millionaire" who was working in Bodrum.

I have seldom been so happy to see anybody. I had not the ability to make archaeological drawings, nor could I teach Mustafa to make them, since I did not know exactly what was required. Mustafa and I pressured Kemal to invite John and Honor on our trip to Yassi Ada in search of the "heaps of pots" south of the island. He agreed with great reluctance, because he was afraid of what his wife would say and because, as he said,

"Women are bad luck on boats, especially pretty ones."

A woman diver was so wildly exotic to the people of Bodrum, whose women were mostly locked up and whose marriageable girls were never seen in public, that they had in some way to justify such scandalous behavior. This was done by treating Honor as a member of whatever sex she happened to be with. She drank with us and the sponge divers, always going home when things began to get really boozy. Next day she could be seen giggling with a circle of village women on her visit to the village bath. She achieved, in short, what can only be defined as bisexual status, no mean feat in a regular Moslem community.

Her freedom did not inspire village women to seek it for themselves. To them she belonged in a class with the legendary females of history, and with Virginia Grace, the archaeologist in Athens who was identifying amphoras for us. I had talked about Miss Grace so much and with such enthusiasm that Captain Kemal and his men had begun to refer to her as "O wise broken pot woman," and to invoke her name in arguments.

Honor's greatest accolade came finally from Captain Kemal. His wife began to scold him for "that blonde you've been carrying around in your boat." Kemal replied simply, "She's a diver." Nothing more was said.

For a few days the weather continued bad, and we wandered around ancient Halicarnassus and tinkered with gear until one evening Captain Kemal announced that we would leave the next day. When we left, the sun was beginning to tint the storm clouds pink in the east. Lightning flashed and the wind boxed the compass, blowing cold eddies down the backs of our necks.

Once again we anchored off the teahouse with columns. A dozen old men greeted us as we came under the arbor. As we sat down, John Carswell remarked that the columns were like ones that he had seen in the Palace of Minos at Knossos, which must have supported in their time an arbor very much like this.

The wind died as the sun rose. As the boat swung to the heading that would take us toward the Karabaglar Islands, I noticed a new addition to our crew. Well on the wrong side of fifty, he wore a canvas jacket and ragged trousers of rough country tweed. He had a three-day growth of beard. One foot hung at an awkward angle and he limped, hanging on to the main boom in order to stand upright. Kemal had told us about this old diver. His name was Ahmet, but they called him Shaitan (Devil) because only the devil or a man in league with him could have had so many diving escapes.

Devil was friendly. He immediately began telling Mustafa about piles of amphoras, a huge heap of tiles as big as washboards, underwater ruins, and other things. Mustafa translated bits of his talk in the intervals when he hesitated in order to recall things seen twenty and thirty years ago. Devil had worked everywhere that sponge boats go: Tripoli, Tunisia, the Greek islands, mainland Greece, and off Africa, where there are no harbors and the Kalymnos fleet lies at night in the open sea to long anchor warps, and men don't walk on land for months on end. He had shipped with Kemal south to Iskenderun and north to the Dardanelles in the days before the war. He and Mustafa spoke a mixture of Greek and Turkish unintelligible to anyone but themselves.

We rounded Hussein Point and stood directly for Yassi Ada, on the same course that we had held when

bucking the *meltem* on our previous trips. Now I
leaned over the bows watching the bow wave as we
slid over a sea so smooth that it took an effort of imagination to believe that great waves had ever disturbed its
calm surface.

They dressed Ali, one of the younger divers, for
the first dive. When we came under the west reef of
Yassi Ada he dropped over. We waited, anxiously studying his bubbles. He surfaced to say that he could not
find the wreck. With a grunt of disgust, Captain Kemal
began dressing himself. He splashed over the side. With
Ali at the tiller responding to directions from Kiasim,
who squatted with the lifeline in the angle of the bows,
we zigzagged for ten minutes, working parallel to the
island. Then there was a series of jerks on the lifeline,
and Kiasim shouted.

"Here!"

We dropped a fisherman's buoy, a gourd with a cord
wrapped around it so that it would unwind, with a piece
of scrap iron for an anchor. The gourd spun madly for a
couple of minutes, then stopped and began drifting off
to leeward. The cord had jammed. By this time we
were far off the place. Kemal surfaced, furious. He
grabbed the tiller while they dressed Devil and ran the
boat up to the exact spot. Devil's "on the bottom" signal
was followed by the rapid jerks that told us he was on
the wreck.

I dropped overboard. Far below I could see the bubbles from Devil's exhaust valve. I followed his lifeline
down. When I reached bottom, I shook hands with
Devil, who seemed glad to see me. My depth gauge read
a hundred and twenty feet. Devil pointed vaguely off to
what seemed like a large rock formation thirty feet or so

away. I swam toward it, and halfway there realized that the stones were amphoras. They were round and very big, not my idea of what amphoras should look like. They seemed more like the eggs of some sea monster.

Smaller, onion-shaped ones lay among them. I picked a small one off the edge of the pile and pulled it free of the mud. I was surprised that it came very easily. I held it upright, and a stream of sand poured out. When the sand stopped, I took a deep breath, removed the mouthpiece, and put it under the mouth of the jar. No air came. I rolled over on my back and tried again. Air bubbled out of the mouthpiece and into the mouth of the jar. A shower of mud, sand, and small stones spewed out. I thought, suddenly, that I was being damn foolish. What if a lump of mud fell out of the jar and clogged the mouthpiece, leaving me to free escape from over a hundred feet? I replaced the mouthpiece and took a cautious breath, thankful for the familiar ring as the air came.

Devil held out a line. I grabbed it, pulled one of the smaller jars off the pile, and tied it on, remembering to get the rope looped around the neck of the jar so that the weight would not bear against a single fragile handle.

I swam up and over the wreck, after waving thanks to Devil. There seemed to be no orderly stacking of the jars, which lay close together within an oblong which seemed about right for a fair-sized cargo ship. My air began to come hard and I pulled the reserve.

When I was twenty feet above the wreck I saw one of the big round amphoras falling from above, spinning as it fell. A plume of mud streamed from its mouth. Like a heavily protected soccer goalie, Devil was trying to field it. It struck the slope a few yards from him and bounced down into deeper water, as the diver waved his hands in ineffectual slow motion.

Mustafa was waiting in the dinghy, looking grim. He said that Rasim was sick, very sick. I swam over to the ship. Rasim, the refugee engineer, was sitting on the hatch looking green and shaky, but otherwise all right. I asked him what had happened, wondering if it had anything to do with Devil's crazy football game.

Rasim had gotten off just after me. Like me, he had followed Devil's bubbles down until he had seen the wreck. He picked one of the big amphoras off the pile, dragged it over to Devil, and handed it to him to hold so that he could fill it with air. When he let go of the amphora, Devil dropped it. Rasim picked it up and handed it to him again. Devil threw it away again. Rasim mumbled "To hell with it," propped the amphora bottom up, and filled it full of air while Devil watched, fascinated. When it began to float, Rasim swam gently upwards, holding the jar upright by the handles so that the air would not spill out of it.

As the air expanded, a cloud of sand boiled out of the jar and its speed increased. Then it began to rock wildly back and forth. By this time Rasim could not tell down from up, as the water was clouded with mud from the jar, which flipped over and sank, dragging him down. He let go and watched it. Then, furious, he swam after it, grabbed it, and tried to turn it over. By this time he was nearly on the bottom again and almost out of air. He dropped the jar and headed up. When he surfaced, he had an attack of giddiness and almost passed out.

Devil came up the ladder grinning, and remarked that he had enjoyed Rasim's dance. He had been waiting for him to be knocked out by variations of pressure. Then he apologized to Rasim for not understanding what he had wanted. He had tied another jar to the lifeline, and we pulled it up. Onion-shaped, it flashed with brilliant red and yellow marine growths which would fade as the jar dried.

Captain Kemal headed the boat toward Marilyn Monroe island, where we would anchor for lunch. Halfway over, Devil, still in the suit with only his helmet off, complained of pains in his knees and spine. Kemal clapped the helmet on him again and dropped him overboard to recompress.

No one spoke. Kemal and the diver Ali sat together in the stern, looking at me and then at the amphoras. Ali glowered when his eyes met mine. A hundred feet below us, alone in the cold water, Devil was sweating out his bends, in no pain with the protecting pressure around him, but knowing that death or paralysis might be waiting for him on the surface.

The water was still deep blue, and very beautiful. It was very hot. We rolled heavily in the open channel. John Carswell, unused to boats, chose that moment to be miserably, violently seasick, then slumped, grayfaced, in the port scuppers. Honor dipped her handkerchief in the sea and wiped his forehead.

I decided to start the compressor, but no sooner had I wrapped the rope around the flywheel than Rasim curtly ordered me to stop, in a voice that could not be argued with. He pulled out a sack and spread it over the amphoras we had raised.

Mustafa explained quietly that Kemal was giving Devil five minutes of recompression time for every fathom. The captain came over to me and asked if I knew anything better. I shook my head. I did know something better, but how could I explain then that decompression diving tables, the diving times permissible at every depth, have been accurately calculated, or that correct recompression of a bent diver took a minimum of twelve hours and could never safely be done by rule of thumb? We had no diving tables.

"The fool should quit," said Kemal. "He has been diving for thirty-five years. No other job. No land. The *manjura* money all went for raki. He is nearly sixty years old and I don't like to take him, but what can I do? He comes and begs. I used to work for him when I began with Ali Kaptan, when Devil was first diver in Bodrum. What would you do, Peter, what would you do?"

The captain looked off at Yassi Ada, across the glassy water. I shook my head, and patted his knee. He stood up and offered me a cigarette. The tension eased a little. There were no more accusing glances at me. The ship's boy cut some tomatoes, slopped some oil over them, and handed us the plate. We sopped oil from the pan with black bread and thought of the little bubbles in a man's blood, and the fearful mystery, explained in dozens of volumes yet not fully understood by anybody, of "the bends."

We brought Devil up once. He still complained. Ali and Kemal rubbed his hands for a minute, clapped the helmet on again, and sent him down to ride the half broomstick for three more hours.

The sun was falling behind Kos when we got him back on deck, paralyzed with cold, but all right. We ran into big Karabaglar and anchored for the night. Kiasim cooked up a delicious pot of thick soup, but no one was hungry. We were more interested in raki.

That night I dreamed about the bends. When people found out that I was a diver they always asked about sharks and sea monsters, I suppose because it is more interesting to battle a shark than to be paralyzed from the waist down.

In the morning Honor and I dived on the wreck with the globe-shaped amphoras, Wreck III, the third wreck we had found at Yassi Ada. The Turks were amazed. They had never seen a woman dive before. In the afternoon we showed her the west reef, the first site that we had discovered. She found a Roman lamp with an illegible inscription on its base at the bottom of the main heap of broken amphoras.

But John and Honor had to go on with their tour, and Rasim's vacation was over. So after two days of measuring, photographing, and attempting to make drawings of the Yassi Ada complex, we headed back to Bodrum.

VII

~~~~~

Down the Coast

KEMAL WAS headed south. It took a week to pack
Mandalinche with the extra gear and stores for several months at sea. Although we would never be more
than half a mile off shore, the coast was deserted and
without stores. There were sacks of *paximadia*, ordinary
bread baked twice to make hardtack; jars of homemade
dried and salted meat which was half rotten when the
time came to eat it; baskets of tomatoes and peppers;
and cartons of Bafra cigarettes, rumored to be made
from the sweepings of a first-class cigarette factory in
Izmir.

Evenings we spent in the *gasinosu* with Kemal and
other captains and divers. The most successful raconteur
was a lithe young diver named Ahmet, who worked for
mad Ibrahim, one of Kemal's rivals. He told incredible
dirty stories which always involved buggery. Once I
tried to counter by telling a heterosexual story, and all
the men were shocked. I realized that I had broken a
taboo of some kind.

Mustafa produced a dozen brightly colored stocking
caps and presented each of us with one with great cere-

mony. The men wore them with pride. Kemal began to introduce us as "divers who can go forty fathoms" to amazed *gasinosu* audiences of yokels, who wore flat caps and homespun suits cut to the latest village style, that of the early 1930's.

Mustafa translated some overheard comments:

"Do you mean they can actually dive? But they're rich, they don't have to!"

"The tall one is an *American?*"

"Really? What does he eat?"

We were not unhappy when, early one morning, we chugged past the Pasha's tomb on the point, bound for Knidos across the Keramic Gulf from Bodrum. We anchored at dusk behind the ancient breakwater. Nothing remained in Knidos of the famous temple of Demeter, and the place was inhabited only by a squad of surly coastguardmen, assigned to keep watch for Greek fishermen poaching Turkish waters, from a shack on Cape Krio cobbled together from the ruins of the temple of Apollo. Kiasim squinted out at the heaps of marble blocks as he stirred the soup, and remarked that Knidos marble made good lime.

Long after I left Turkey I met a Greek captain who had learned his trade in schooners, hauling marble from Knidos to the Dodecanese islands. The trade had providentially been stopped in 1912, when the Dodecanese were ceded to Italy. Families who had grown rich from the boom in the sponge trade were then building big houses in Symi and Kalymnos, and would eventually have destroyed what was left of the ruins of Knidos.

The archons of ancient Knidos, whose stamps on the handles of Knidian amphoras found all over the ancient world attest their city's interest in the wine trade, would have been amused by the twist of economic fate that had caused the marble of their city, bought with the proceeds of the wine trade, to become its only export.

We were soon gathered around a canvas spread on the fo'c'sle, dipping out of a communal pot of bean soup. The captain, divers, Mustafa, and I ate at the head of the table before the others. The seamen sat below the salt at the after end of the forehatch, not presuming to dip in until we had eaten our fill. The two ship's boys hung in the background and ate the greasy leavings after the others had finished. I curled up in the sleeping place that Kiasim had assigned me beside the anchor chain in the portside scupper, and was instantly asleep.

We were underway before the sun broke. Captain Kemal was the first diver down, and he showed his good will by sending up an amphora neck from a heap of smashed sherds at the foot of the ancient breakwater. As the morning wore on and we moved around the cape, every diver sent up something — amphora necks, halves of broken bowls, pieces of corroded copper pots. Knidos was an underwater junkyard. After the first hour I had to ask them only to pick up material when it seemed to come from a "wreck," a place where there was a heap of identical pottery, because we had no room on board and there was too much to draw in the time we had available.

I swam with my mask among the ruins scattered in the shallow water off the point, and along the ancient mole, which was built of huge stones that must weigh more than twenty or thirty tons each. I wondered how the ancient builders had handled them.

In the afternoon one of the divers remembered a

heap of jars on a sandy bottom twenty fathoms deep around the point under the cape. Mustafa rowed me to the point. Ten feet out from the greenish shallows, the sea turned the dark blue that signals deep water.

Because it feels better when diving alone in a place like that to have something in one's hand, I grabbed the spear gun and rolled backwards off the stern. The air sang sweetly through the regulator and into the mouthpiece. Thirty feet below, a ledge projected ten feet from the cliff. I could see nothing beyond it but the indigo of deep water. To one side there was a cleft in the rock. I swam over the abyss, and followed it down, planing toward a ledge that materialized as I glided down feeling weightless as a bird.

I brought up on the ledge and saw the "pile of amphoras" that "looked like stones" a little below me. I swam down, excited, but found that it was really a pile of stones, inhabited by half a dozen groupers who lay there and looked at me, twiddling their fins. I speared the biggest. The depth gauge read a hundred and ten feet.

The sand began forty feet below. I swam down to it and headed right around the cliff. If there were a wreck there it would lie in the sand at the bottom of the slope. It was time to talk to myself:

"Keep your head, boy, keep your head. It's deep down here. You ain't sober even if you think you are . . ."

The narcosis of deep water often has the same effect as alcohol. It can lead a diver into thinking that he is superhuman, while his actual performance is reduced to the idiot level.

"You're just a slob, buddy, keep watching, don't go too fast . . ."

The depth gauge read a hundred and eighty feet. The sand sloped off to infinity at an ever steeper angle. I was tempted to swim down it. A big grouper came up, decided I was a bore, and left. My watch said I'd been down twenty minutes. Enough. After a decent decompression time at ten feet, I surfaced beside the boat.

The day was almost over. Kemal steered *Mandalinche* into the harbor behind the ancient breakwater and we anchored for the night in water so clear that, standing on the deck, I could see the anchor on the bottom fifteen feet below. I took my mask and fins and jumped over the side. Kiasim waved at me from the stern, where he was cooking grouper soup with beans and rice.

The sandy bottom was covered with a thick mat of weed that looked like green wheat bending under a steady breeze. A shape caught my eye, what was left of a small caïque. Her timbers were burned, and I wondered if she had been here for the night like us, cooking dinner, and had caught fire. The wood was very rotten where it was not protected by charcoal. In some places only the burned parts remained, forming a queer tracery that I could pull apart with my fingers. Where I swished away the sand, using my hand as a kind of broom, the timbers were like new. In a few years all that was visible of the little ship would disappear, leaving her bottom planks safely covered, to last forever along with everything else that lies buried in Knidos harbor.

Every wreck has its grouper and this wreck, being small, had a small grouper. In the twenty years or so that it would take him to reach full growth, the wreck would disappear. He worked himself into an impracticable crevice, one that was no defense against anything. I winked at him and snapped my fingers. He flicked his tail and swam away.

During the month that followed we found hundreds of underwater sites. A few were on sand or mud which had preserved bits of ship timbers, but most were scattered heaps of badly broken pottery concreted to the rock. It was easy to find material, but impossible to cope with the incredible quantities of broken pottery that we had no space to store and no time to draw. It was hard to decide, with so little time, whether two or three broken amphoras of identical type indicated a shipwreck or were just odd jars heaved into the water after a party, or as an offering to Poseidon from some captain whistling up a wind. We tried to select what might be meaningful and ignored the rest.

Our commonest finds were amphoras, and the types we found, when the drawings were checked against Miss Grace's master file in Athens, made an interesting commentary on the ancient commerce of that part of the coast. Only one out of ten jars was older than the time of Alexander the Great. The trade boom which appears to have occurred after the Romans stopped piracy and promoted trade was reflected in the high percentage of first century B.C. to second century A.D. amphoras we found. Jars from the period when the Roman Empire fell apart in the third, fourth, and fifth centuries were rare, but amphoras of the booming early years of the Byzantine Empire formed the largest group of all. We had neither the time nor knowledge nor funds to raise and draw the thousands of jars necessary for valid historical conclusions, but our skimming of the surface gave an idea of the possibilities of such a survey.

I became more and more convinced of the necessity of

the guidance of sponge divers on such surveys. It was difficult to find underwater sites which they remembered even when one was within a hundred yards of the spot. In deep water there was little chance of finding a wreck unless one knew the exact spot. This was brought home to me at Arap Adasi, where Ahmet Erbil had found the famous Demeter bronze. Mustafa and I mulled over the chart which we had made from Erbil's description of his find, and decided that there were only two possible places where the ship bearing the Demeter could have struck. The first was a black cliff at the mouth of the bay, with deep water all around. The cliff fell sheer to where the rocks began at one hundred and fifty feet. Feeling like a fly on a wall in the clear water, I finned down to the rock pile. The sand of the true ocean bottom was visible down the slope. When I reached it I saw, beyond the last boulders, an object sticking out of the sand. It was twice as tall as I, big around as my arm, and covered with limestone sea-growth. On its top grew a round, fat, greenish black sponge, which I pulled off. Suddenly the tall object groaned and fell with a ponderous thump, nearly catching me under it. Bubbles poured from the broken stump. It was iron, turned into something like mushy soft coal by the chemical action of the sea.

I saw a movement out of the corner of my eye. A grouper, nearly as long as I and a lot broader, was watching me. His mouth was inquiringly agape and I could see the rows of small pointed teeth. I aimed my spear at the juncture of brain and spinal cord, and thought better of it. I was alone and very deep, and if I lost the spear we would be without fish for days. He came so close that the spear point touched the vital spot; then he backed off, and went on staring.

When my air gave out I hung on the stop, pondering the near impossibility of finding anything at such a depth with only one or two divers when we did not know exactly where to look. We shifted our search to the harbor behind the island (Arap Adasi means Black Island) and found hundreds of different types of broken amphoras, evidence that the place had been used as an anchorage in ancient times.

The days ran together. When the sun was high, it beat down onto the shadeless deck where we crouched, hungry and half asleep except for those whose duty kept them awake. The engine always chugged at quarter throttle. Its vibration made a ring of concentric circles on the smooth surface of the surrounding sea. The compressor's belt slapped every time it hit the high place on the oak-shod drive wheel. The clatter of our worn-out machinery echoed off the mountains, making eagles fly and startling herds of goats. We had long since ceased to notice it.

I learned that when the captain, cross-legged on the dressing bench, glanced at the clock and at the boil of bubbles breaking the surface of the water, spat, shifted the lifeline from his right hand to his left and dug into his pocket for a cigarette, there was time to relax before the next dive. When he flipped his cigarette into the sea and stood up, everyone woke up. The man at the tiller did something to the engine, its tone deepened, and the ship eased up to the bubbles. Swaying, bare toes digging into the deck, the captain took up the slack, then jerked hard three times. Samy, the ship's boy, leaped from where he was crouched in the shadow of the cabin and ran to release the rope that held the hinged diving ladder out of the water. A diver coiled the hose, taking care to keep the coils neat on the rack. Twenty feet away, the gleaming copper helmet broke the surface in a froth of foam. Like pulling in a played-out fish, Captain Kemal drew the diver to the surface.

When his helmet and breastplate rose over the bulwark, the men rushed to get him on board. One twisted the helmet and lifted it off his head. Another released the big lead weights. The boy heaved the bulging net sponge bag over the bulwark and dumped its contents into the scuppers. A dozen sponges might gleam shiny and black, the size and shape of cannon balls, and with them the neck and handles of an ancient amphora.

The silent rhythm of ceremonial preparations for a dive never changed. Occasionally when something went wrong on the bottom and a diver felt that his tenders were at fault, there would be cursing when the helmet came off. This was the only time it was permissible to lose one's temper. Once the belt connecting the compressor to the engine began slipping, unnoticed by anybody. Kemal, over a hundred feet below, signaled that he wanted to come up. When he was undressed he raged through the boat, boxing ears. I cringed inconspicuously in the scuppers, ashamed as the rest of them. A year later I learned that that was how a good friend of Kemal's had died.

"There is no margin of error on a sponge boat," Captain Kemal said in the *gasinosu* months later. "All old divers know this, and the young ones who don't learn it fast never grow old."

The restrictions and customs which shaped sponge-boat life all hinged on the fact, difficult to see at first or even to imagine, that diving was a dice game played against the sea. We were always hungry because Kemal and the other divers believed that eating during the diving day brought on the bends, and we killed our hunger with cigarettes. If our hungry bellies growled, we felt we were doing something to load the dice our way. The rice and beans that we usually had for our one meal of the day could not replace calories lost during a day's diving, and we all got thinner as the weeks passed.

As we got thinner, we dived better and better. At the beginning of the trip I had been unable to dive with a mask to more than thirty or forty feet. At the end, when I was so tired on deck that it was an effort to read or write and an exhausting job to start my air compressor, I could get to eighty feet or more with ease, and always felt good in the water.

The worst time for me was early morning. Long before light, the ship's boys would pull the net bags full of the previous day's sponges out of the water and flop them on the foredeck beside me. Groaning wearily and aching all over from rolling onto the anchor chain, I would pull my blankets out of the mess and sit on the bulwark while the crew crawled out of their cubbyholes and began cleaning sponges.

These were round if they had come from a sandy bottom, irregular if they had been picked off rocks. The night before, the barefoot boys had trampled the fresh sponges to remove living sponge organisms, which were milky and acrid-smelling. When Honor had wrinkled her nose Kemal smiled and remarked that he enjoyed it. It smelled, he said, like money.

The squeezed sponges would have rotted out overnight in the net bags hung alongside *Mandalinche*. Now the golden skeletons showed through the gray of the worn nets. Each had to be pounded on the deck until the remaining black matter was removed, along with the animals that had lived in the sponge: tiny indignant crabs, baby shrimps, miniature lobsters, and several kinds of worms.

The boys did the first hard, dirty work of dipping the sponges into a bucket of water and smashing them to the deck so that the water, rushing out of the holes in the sponge, carried the extraneous matter with it. Kemal and Kiasim gave the last pound, flicked the last flecks of black off with their knives, and rammed the clean sponges into one of the sacks lashed in the port shrouds.

When the heap of sponges that covered the foredeck was under control, Kiasim would go to tinker with the engine. After suitable curses, clanks, and bangs, he would shout for someone to turn the flywheel. The one-lunger would burp, and clouds of foul-smelling black smoke would pour out of the after hatch until the engine caught and ran away, very fast, out of control, shooting smoke rings out of the exhaust pipe. At this point Kemal always cursed Kiasim just as the old man emerged on deck to grab the throttle and steady the engine to the endless thumping throb that would shake us all day.

This was coffee-wanting time. The divers didn't drink coffee on principle. In any case there *was* no coffee, because the government had decided that importing coffee used up valuable foreign exchange and that the people would be as well off with tea. As a substitute I lit Bafras one after the other and sat out of the way, dreaming about fat crisp Yankee doughnuts, Nescafé with canned milk, big metal coffeemakers in roadside diners, and Cappucino with foamy cream on top. By the time I could sneak a tomato and a bit of hardtack without being too conspicuous, the first diver was usually down, with Kemal tending the lifeline while one of the boys paid out the frayed hose, chanting the depths as the hand went up on the pressure gauge attached to the cabin front.

The weather was usually calm, as the *meltem*, the northwest summer wind, was cut off by the land under which we were working, and by ten we were usually gasping from the heat reflected from the cliffs and the glassy sea. The young men would peel off their shirts and work in their underwear, knee-length bloomers of heavy blue cloth. The older men always kept on their skintight woolen shirts. On these days, when I jumped over the side with mask and fins to spear fish and explore the shallow waters of the coastline, the water was so clear that I could see the diver over a hundred feet below, dragging the air hose in a long loop behind him. The bubbles from his helmet expanded as they rose until they were as big as silver melons, which popped and multiplied into smaller bubbles when I touched them with my spear. The younger men all swam, clumsily but enthusiastically. Kemal only swam once. He had a hard time with my mask and fins and handed them back after a few minutes with a hopeless grin, saying that he was too old for such foolishness.

The coast was full of ruined villages, uninhabited except for coast guards with ancient rifles and dirty uniforms, and savage-looking goatherds who stood stockstill like deer about to run. They stared, sometimes for hours, until we passed. These villages had been inhabited by Greeks, who had fled or been massacred by the Turks at the time of the great exodus of 1922. No one had resettled them, for the country was poor, fruitful only for those who could farm the sea. The Turks, land-bound by tradition except for small groups like the Bodrum men, could not survive there.

The rocks were full of fish and octopus, which I stopped catching when I found that Kiasim, Mustafa, and I were the only ones who would eat it. The valleys often had orchards run wild, and we gorged ourselves on fresh figs, the best I had ever eaten. Dried figs had been an important export to Rome from Halicarnassus in ancient times. Now only we and the shepherds ate them, leaving the rest for the birds. We never discovered any onions, which the Knidians exported in quantity in Caesar's day.

In the evenings we anchored in tiny bays with the stern moored to a handy tree. There we cooked and ate our meal of the day, then sat around the driftwood fire listening to stories from Kemal or Kiasim until it was time to sleep. We learned the men's names, where they came from, and why they were diving. Devil, the oldest, had been diving for over thirty years. He was a sweet-natured man, stupid, half crazy with having had the bends so often, and not much use as a diver. Kemal always treated him with respect, perhaps in memory of the old days when they had worked together. Devil had a hard time feeding his eight living children.

Mehmet was fifty, and Aidedoo, one of the boys, was his son. Aidedoo swore that he would never dive. The only young and able man on board was Ali, only thirty-seven and a top diver. We were a crew of the too old and too young, one of the last three sponge crews in Bodrum. During the trip nearly everyone asked Mustafa if he could help them find a job in Izmir. Kiasim said that he would be willing to work as a doorkeeper. Samy, the youngest boy, wanted to learn a trade. Only Kemal did not talk about quitting. He took pleasure in command, in his little ship, in his place at the head of the canvas in the evenings, and in the steady flow of sponges from starboard to port in the early mornings.

For all the sour talk, there was a difference between the Bodrum men and the shore people that we met on the way. Though on the surface good Turks and true Moslems, the Carian sailors had a style of their own. Speculations about atavistic survivals are wrong more often than not, but it is difficult to deny that there has been a continuing tradition of sea roving in the villages around Bodrum since the beginning. The legendary King Minos in the second millenium before Christ is said to have expelled the Carians from the Aegean islands because of their incorrigible piracy. Scylax, the first man to cross the Indian Ocean, came from a village near Bodrum. It was hard to evoke those forgotten seamen, but the hard boot-leather faces and defiant eyes with deep crinkles around them, the faded red sashes, baggy canvas pants tied at the knees, and the rag turbans on the heads of *Mandalinche*'s crew conjured easy images of the Barbary corsairs.

Turgut, Barbarossa's great lieutenant in the time of Solyman the Magnificent, came from near Bodrum. He was killed during the siege of Malta, fighting the Knights of Rhodes, the same crusaders who had built St. Peter's castle in Bodrum and given the town its modern name. Turgut reincarnated would feel at home on the deck of any Bodrum sponge boat, once he got used to the engine, and it is no coincidence that the local school is named after him.

In Istanbul, a young man in a sharp double-breasted suit and pointed shoes, one of the generation grown up since Ataturk, had warned me to be careful, that the coast people were not real Turks at all, but smugglers contaminated by the neighboring Greeks. Stackleberg, who had some dealings with pirates on the coast in the early nineteenth century, said that they had a very mixed religion. Nominally Turks, they kept a candle burning before an ikon of St. Nicholas in the main cabin, and were in league with Greek Orthodox priests, who acted as spies for them and took a commission on the loot.

The answer is perhaps that the Turks of the coast were and are much closer to the Greeks of the Dodecanese than to the Turks of the interior, and that what I was seeing was the last flicker of an individuality of character that had existed intact until the thirteenth century, when the Seljuk Turks captured the region and converted the villagers to the Moslem faith. The towns of the coast face Greece and the Aegean. Now the coast is dead, because of the closed Greek-Turkish sea frontiers. Trade by which the coastal villagers lived has stopped. Ataturk, the modernizer of twentieth-century Turkey, established the policy which aims to turn the coastal people away from the Greek Aegean and toward Ankara. In a few years the roads through the mountains to Ankara will be finished, and the children of *Mandalinche*'s men will soon be indistinguishable from their compatriots in the capital.

One evening we stopped diving an hour before dark and headed down the coast at our full speed of six knots toward a great cape. Kemal concealed our compressor and tanks under a canvas tarpaulin. I was allowed to stand on deck but had to take my glasses off. Without them I passed well enough for one of the crew. There was a coast guard station on that cape, and Kemal and all the crew were dead afraid of the coast guard or of anyone in uniform. Mustafa and I had letters but, as Mustafa put it, letters meant little to a man who could not read, and who was armed both with a rifle and the conviction that all foreigners were spies.

We anchored under the cape at the entrance to Marmarice bay, out of sight of the coast guards. The men called the cape Kadirga Feneri (Frigate Point), a curious survival from when the British fleet under Nelson waited there in January and February of 1800 before the Battle of Aboukir.

We ran out of water. Kemal and Devil discussed the whereabouts of the nearest spring. The old man swore on his honor that we would find water in the next bay. The tired crew went reluctantly to heave up the anchor. At the new anchorage, the older ship's boy, Aidedoo, mocked Devil.

"The old boy is kooky," he said to no one in particular. "We'll never find water in a place like this."

Mehmet headed for shore in the dinghy. Everyone watched Devil, who began to bluster that he was certain that there was water there, because . . . He was cut short by a shout from Mehmet. The spring was dry.

The boy Aidedoo tormented him. "Yah, yah, if there ever was a spring!"

Devil walked aft, groaning. That night I heard him crying.

The prospect of being waterless made us angry, and

we ate our half-cooked beans with peppers and tomatoes, and one lobster to divide among the seven of us, in
silence. In the morning we headed down Marmarice bay,
which could pass for a Norwegian fjord with its pine
cliffs and weird rock formations. We passed a couple
of sponge boats, their captains friends of Kemal. One
of them was working old-style. Although the relays of
pump men had been replaced by a belt to the compressor from the engine, like *Mandalinche*, the boat was kept
over the diver by sweeps. One of the boys rowed over
to him for an amphora full of water, and we dived all
day.

We tied up in Marmarice that evening. Mustafa went
for his mail, while I had a delightful shave. A telegram
was waiting for him which called him back to Izmir.
We spent the evening drinking with Kemal and another
sponge captain, and climbed on the weekly mail boat for
Izmir at the end of the long evening.

The mail boat's brass band played from the first-class
deck to a huge crowd milling on the pier. As they pulled
up the gangway, our last sight of Kemal was when, after
waving us good-by from the dock, he staggered weeping through the crowd with his crew, all in their pirate
caps, trailing behind. We cried too. We had just drunk
nearly a liter of raki each.

A bed without fleas and a European meal would have
been marvelous, but we could not afford it. We awoke
on the Number Four hatch of whatever her name was,
with awful hangovers, covered with flea bites, to be
told by a pig-faced steward that third-class passengers
were not allowed into the second-class lounge for morning tea.

VIII

∽∽∽∽∽

The Bends

WE ARRIVED in Izmir covered with welts, our stomachs suffering from the third-class hospitality of the Turkish Sea Monopoly, but essentially happy. Our notebooks were full of information about wrecks. Hakki Bey was pleased. There was a letter from Miss Grace in Athens, who said that Honor Frost had come to see her and had shown her the Yassi Ada drawings. The shallow wreck on the west reef could be dated to the first century A.D. Duplicate amphoras had been found in Pompeii. The deep wrecks at Yassi Ada were late Roman, fourth to seventh century A.D.

Soon we were on the battered country bus again, on our way back to Bodrum. We hoped to catch Kemal on his return from Marmarice, before he left on his last big trip of the year, as he had promised to show us other wrecks, near Bodrum. In any case, we needed to learn much more about the Yassi Ada deep wrecks. How much of the hulls were left? How big were they? And who knew what might lie nearby? Yassi Ada was certainly the richest wreck rock yet found in the Mediterranean.

As usual, the bus was miserable. The pain was alleviated by a wonderful argument that took place at about the halfway mark, when a village woman tried to push an old man out of her way in order to fit her massive behind into the crowded bench. The old man's wife accused the lady, in a loud voice heard by all, of making a shameless attempt to seduce her husband.

"That broken stick of a man!" replied the accused woman. "Why, it's lucky he has you to take care of him. The poor old boy couldn't do a thing even if I was a movie star!"

His wife defended him. "You'd be surprised what he can do!"

This went on for half an hour, interrupted by roars of laughter from the other passengers. It ended when the old boy began beating his wife, and the driver had to intervene.

Things weren't so cheerful in Bodrum. We piled our gear in the hotel, and went to look for Kemal. We found him sitting with Kiasim in the *gasinosu*, a half-empty raki bottle in front of them. The place was empty, a bad sign. It meant that Kemal was in a mean mood and people were afraid to sit nearby.

That afternoon mad Ibrahim's boat had come into the harbor with a badly bent diver, who had been caught at a hundred feet for over two hours when his hose had tangled on some rocks. It was Ahmet, the raconteur. He was a good friend of Kemal's.

At the hospital we found him groaning, half unconscious, paralyzed from the waist down. His wife was crouched in a corner, her shawl over her head. The doctor told us that he was giving him X-ray treatments.

"Couldn't we send him to the navy recompression chamber in Istanbul?" I asked.

The doctor turned on me. "Are you a doctor?"

I confessed that I was not, but that I was sure that the only cure for paralytic bends was recompression. The doctor smiled. If we wanted to take the responsibility, he would be glad to turn the patient over to us, but . . .

We walked back to the *gasinosu* and drank, dully, thinking of the man who was going to die, or at the very least be hopelessly crippled for life, for lack of a competent doctor and a recompression chamber. I wanted to shout, to scream, to protest.

There might have been a very slight chance of saving Ahmet, if we could hire a taxi for the trip to Izmir, and if we could find a plane in Izmir to fly him to Istanbul in time. But if he died on the way it was certain that we would be blamed, first by the doctor and then by his family and all Bodrum.

We discussed the possibilities of action, and came to the terrible conclusion that without the doctor's cooperation, we could not risk the desperate journey to Istanbul. Many divers have died in Bodrum through incompetent medical treatment. It was nearly certain that Ahmet was going to die. If he did so in a recompression chamber in Istanbul, it would reduce still further the chance of more hopeful cases being sent there.

We labored at conversation. Mustafa made a joke. No one laughed. I tried to tell a story about New York, for Kemal liked hearing about New York. Kemal's men came under the arbor one by one, said "Merhaba," and sat beside us. Kiasim filled their glasses and they drank without enthusiasm.

Captain Kemal waved his hand and looked around as if for someone to challenge the statement that he was about to make. "In those days we were divers. I mean *divers!* Where are the good divers now?" He looked toward Kiasim, who nodded. "I'll tell you where they are!"

He extended his hand and made an ugly gesture, that of piling earth on a grave, one of those shallow graves out by the Mindus Gate past the old wall, which shocked the English archaeologist Newton so badly, because wild dogs and jackals came to dig up and feed on the corpses. Today you can still see human bones there, sticking out of the earth after a rainfall.

Kiasim looked at the dirty floor. His lined face was expressionless, and he looked old and tired. "The lucky ones, ah the lucky ones. Do you know where they are? Eating cheese in the villages, and you can't get them out with dynamite."

I thought of the ones who were neither safely under the ground nor secure on their poor farms, of Devil's pathetic attempts to recapture his lost courage and burnt-out strength, mocked by boys like Aidedoo, begging for a place, giving up at last because no captain would have him any more, and hanging around the cafe on Fridays.

"Do you remember Ab-I-Din?" said Kemal.

Kiasim nodded and halted the piece of watermelon that was on its way to his mouth. "Aaah, Ab-I-Din." The sad old face grew sadder, remembering the days of the *manjuras*, and all the good men in shallow graves on desert islands from Canakkale to Iskenderun.

Kemal turned to me. "Peter, you never saw a man like that. He was black like a new sponge. Shiny. His shoulders were like that." He spread his arms wide.

"And his wrists were like that." The captain grasped his leg just above the knee.

"He could open a bottle like *that*." Kiasim, at the cue, picked up the raki bottle and showed me how Ab-I-Din used to push the cork right into it. They both smiled, remembering, perhaps, a happy binge with Ab-I-Din.

"That man was immune to bends," said Kemal. "Immune, I tell you. Why, once in Benghazi they hit a bank, on a Kalymnos boat. Thirty-five fathoms. Ab-I-Din tied the lifeline onto a rock so they couldn't pull him up. He strung so many sponges on it that it took two of them to get it up. He untied it after forty minutes, and came up like a rocket. The Greek captain said to him, 'Ab-I-Din, you are going to get bent.' Ab-I-Din laughed and said that he was no Greek. He got twenty-six kilos on that dive. Twenty-six kilos.

"You know," Kemal continued, "on those boats we always used to compete for the place of top diver. Ab-I-Din killed a lot of Greeks that way, because he was immune to bends. They would try to match his dives, and whoops!" He made the ugly burying gesture again. "If you never saw that man dive, you wouldn't believe it. I saw him make five fifteen-minute dives in forty and forty-five fathoms in one day. He worked more than once at fifty and fifty-five fathoms. All he wanted to do was dive and dive and dive . . ."

I remembered when I had first begun to dive, and how I too did not want to stop, and I thought that this perhaps was the key to my friendship with Kemal, for he, with his orange groves, did not have to dive, nor did I.

Kemal poured himself another drink and pointed at the raki in his glass. "That's what got him. He was drinking more than a liter a day toward the end, and he got thin and potbellied. Lost his appetite. During the last year he never ate more than a little bread and half a plate of beans in a day, just a *meze* for his raki. Ah, Ab-I-Din! Go to Kalymnos and ask the Greeks. When they used to tell him to be careful, he would smile, just as innocent, and say, 'I thought I came here to dive, Captain.'

"And women! When he hit Izmir, he used to lock himself up in one of those places and stay for days, till he was broke and the girls were all worn out. It takes a good man to make one of those girls tired, let alone two or three . . ."

Kiasim said, "There won't be any more like him."

I broke in before the conversation could get side-tracked, and asked what had finally happened to Ab-I-Din.

"It was in a Bozburnu boat. They were on one of those forty-fathom banks, off Cesme, where we used to work a lot with *manjuras*. He came up from fifteen minutes in forty-two fathoms. Told the captain he was bent. They tried to get him to recompress, but he refused. Told them that he knew it was all over for him. They took him to the hospital in Izmir and he died."

Mehmet told me, one day long after this, how in the hospital Ab-I-Din had asked for a little raki. The doctor refused. The captain smuggled a bottle in, and they had a last drink. He was in little pain, but the paralysis rose until he could not breathe any more. He told the captain to say good-by to all his friends, shook hands with the crew, and died. Mehmet remembers that his grip was still strong an hour before the end.

Mehmet came in at midnight. Diver Ahmet was dead. The third raki bottle was empty. We went quietly off to bed. I could not sleep in spite of all the raki. The town generator had long since stopped, so I lit a candle and pulled out my diving manual. How could I explain to the doctor, to Kemal, to the other divers, what it was all about? How could I explain to people at parties who asked me about sharks that sharks are nothing compared to those little bubbles in a man's blood. You can fight a shark, if you see him first, for even though he can swim at thirty knots and cut you in half with one bite, he is a coward and won't fight for his dinner except under very special circumstances. A bubble of nitrogen, on the other hand, has no personality. You can't frighten it. It's just there.

I turned to the diving manual:

During his stay below, the diver breathes air at a pressure higher than the atmospheric, and a certain amount of nitrogen is absorbed by the blood . . . The phenomenon is reversed during the ascent . . . if the ascent is too rapid, the difference between the pressure of the nitrogen dissolved in the various tissues and the hydrostatic pressure may become so great that bubbles begin to form in the blood, as in a bottle of champagne that has just been opened.

These bubbles produce compressed air illness, also known as caisson disease, "the bends," or decompression sickness . . .*

To understand the problem in human terms, go to Kalymnos or Symi or Hydra or Tarpon Springs or Bozburnu or Bodrum. If you sit in any one of the outdoor cafes for the time it takes to drink a Turkish coffee and sip the glass of water that comes with it, you will probably notice a man with a cane shuffling about his mar-

* *The Complete Manual of Free Diving*, pp. 97 ff.

ginal business. If he looks like a seaman, call and ask, "How deep, uncle?"

He will probably reply without looking up, almost as a reflex, "Forty fathoms off Benghazi," or something like, and trundle off, holding his cane like a staff of office. It is. Why should people wonder that sponge divers do not act like boy scouts, when their only merit badge is the cane?

Ask a sponge diver about sea monsters. He will tell you good stories, if you are buying the raki, and laugh at you when you stumble home. Ask him about bends and he will change the subject, unless he knows you very well indeed.

Before I came to Bodrum and began diving in deep water every day, bends were an abstraction, which I knew about but which did not affect me personally. Then I understood. Understood the saintly, resigned, Byzantine ikon look of old divers, and the savage alcoholism of the younger ones. Understood the thing hanging over all of us, never admitted, never mentioned, but there, every day, after every dive. No one makes jokes to a diver just up from a long dive as he surreptitiously feels his back and tries not to show his reaction to that little pain at the belt line, which may mean approaching paralysis or death, but could just as well be a little sprain from heaving too hard on the anchor chain the day before yesterday.

Small symptoms are common. If you struggle to get a sponge out of a crack in a rock on a deep dive, your fingers might ache that evening. If you dive on the decompression tables (if you are a sponge diver, it is not likely that you do), there is still a chance of getting caught, as no table can be one hundred per cent safe

[96]

unless decompression times are prolonged inordinately. Every diving job is a race between the inevitable absorption of nitrogen into the body and time, the time that must be spent on the bottom in order to make money. The unlucky ones get caught.

If it happens to you, you can be paralyzed in your sleep, so that you wake up to find yourself a cripple for life. It can choke you to death, kill you instantly, or twist you into a screaming lump of agony with awful pains in your joints. You might get off with only a headache or an itching rash. Do not feel reassured if you have only minor symptoms. They can be the prelude to agonies which would be the envy of any medieval torturer. If you recover from a bad "bend" you may be afflicted afterwards with a kind of super arthritis, of which the French Navy's Diving Manual remarks: "X-rays reveal extensive decalcification of the extremities of the bones involved; up to the present no treatment has proved effective . . ."

Although the navies of the world have spent millions of dollars on the study of the bends, the malady is still not well understood. Above all, bends are unpredictable. Some sponge divers work for years on the edge of danger and never get caught. Others, like Ahmet or the two who were working off Kadirga Feneri a few years ago, are not so lucky.

The boat off Kadirga Feneri was a *manjura*, with an experienced captain and a good crew. There had never been an accident before the day it happened. They were working on a good bank at thirty fathoms, making ten-minute dives. A few minutes after he came up, one of the divers began to have convulsions. The captain signaled the man who was down to come up immediately, so that the sick diver could be sent down to recompress. By the time the suit was ready for him, the first diver was unconscious. They ran for Marmarice. On the way the second diver, who was sitting on the dressing bench smoking the usual after-dive cigarette, keeled over. He was dead before anyone could reach him. The first man died before they could get to the harbor.

The crew buried their dead, stayed drunk for three days, and went back to work. No one quit.

Outsiders wonder why men put up with this. No one forces them to it, and most could get good jobs ashore. Perhaps the answer lies in the personalities of the divers. Like their ancestors who went out from this coast to man Barbary corsairs, they are fiercely independent and incurably romantic, with a craving for fame and money. When a diver walks down the street in one of the diving towns, people stand aside as he passes. He is somebody.

The best sponges are almost always in deep water along this coast which has been exploited for so long. If men want to make big money, they have to go deep.

Beyond avarice, there is something else in the attraction of deep water. We look down the slope, knowing that it is too deep, and that it is probably no different from the place where we are. We hesitate, thinking of what we might find, curious to see what's down there. Then we go deeper. As narcosis increases, we feel elated, and go deeper still. Someone once remarked to me condescendingly that all we divers really wanted was to return to the womb. He may be right. In deep virgin depths, one feels sometimes as if in the womb of the world.

Every sponge captain and every diver gambles against

the fatal equation. A virgin rock can yield enough sponges in a ten-minute dive to feed a family for a month, or buy half an acre of pasture land. The money is there in deep water, waiting, along with the bends.

The evening after Ahmet died, we were sitting in the cafe. Kemal remarked that what was God's will would happen, and that we were all in the hands of God. I replied that it had nothing to do with God, but with the decompression tables. Giving me the fatherly look that I knew presaged a lecture, he poured me a little raki, passed the bottle around, took a sip of pure raki, and began to talk.

"What do you expect of us? There are at most fourteen working hours in a day. Divers come to dive, not decompress. I contract with my men to give them three dives a day, and we all have families. On a long summer day, the most time all of us together can spend on the bottom is ten hours, and if we make decompression we lose half of that . . . We trust in God."

Mustafa remarked wryly in English, "So instead of killing time, they kill themselves."

Kiasim nodded his head and remarked that God was big, and knew His own mind.

Kemal, a little drunk, said, "This is a great mystery, this thing of the bends."

He did not mean that he did not understand the relationship between the bends and pressure. He understands it very well. But, with one diving suit on board, he has to do the best he can. He does, and has never killed a diver.

The practice in Bodrum, and in all the sponge fleets that I know about, is to recompress a diver immediately if he has a serious symptom. Their way of recompressing is almost exactly like that recommended in the French Navy Diving Manual for circumstances when a recompression chamber is not available:

. . . resubmerge the diver to the depth where he feels relief, but no deeper than 100 feet, and adhere as closely as possible to the rate of ascent given in the following table:

Depth	Rate of ascent in feet per minute
65 feet	2.3
65-30	1.1
30-25	0.8
25-surface	0.5

The Bodrum divers say that the diver ought to go to the depth where he feels relief, and that he should ascend at the rate of one fathom per five minutes. The idea is similar, except that they do not understand that the diver has to spend more time at the shallower stages.

A few years ago, when Kiasim had the bends, Kemal cured him with hot baths, a trick also used by Japanese divers, who swear by it. Apart from a few other simple remedies, and a basic understanding of the problem which varies from captain to captain, the Turkish divers trust in fate, even though they know that something could be done.

The French traveler Sonnini was at Kos in 1777 when the plague broke out. He was amazed that no precautions were taken. Other travelers in the same period were shocked to see the clothing of plague victims sold at public auction in Constantinople. They were told by the Turks: "We trust in God."

IX

~~~~~

Dynamite

IT WAS the end of August, and Bodrum stifled in the
furnace of the Anatolian summer. *Mandalinche*'s one-
lunger had stopped with a crunch a few miles out of
Bodrum, when Kemal was headed north. There were no
engine parts in Turkey, because of the customs, so a new
crankshaft was being made in Izmir. Kemal was restive;
money was going out the window.

Mustafa and I made minor expeditions around Bodrum, swam, explored the town, and spent our evenings
in the cafe with Kemal and his friends. These were as
piratical a set of characters as one could hope for. There
was even a jester, a mad tailor who used to startle me
by poking his forefinger into my chest, looking deep
into my eyes with his own dark black ones blazing out
of his emaciated face, murmuring, "Cosmos, cosmos,
COSMOS!!" He had read Pierre Loti in Turkish, and had
never gotten over it. He believed in divination, ghosts,
devils, and evil spirits, which he claimed to have the
power to exorcise, but over which he occasionally lost
control. The others respected him as a minor prophet
and listened to his ideas about everything. When his

devils were chasing him, his friends always caught and held him, and soothed him with raki.

Captain Hamid, the smuggler, looked and acted like someone out of the *Beggars' Opera*. He was never shaved, was tanned very dark, and had a habit of disappearing without warning from the table, to reappear ten minutes, an hour, or two weeks later, continuing the conversation where it had been interrupted. His main business was smuggling sponges to Greece by way of the Karabaglar Islands, where he would rendezvous with his Greek accomplices. In that tangle of reefs and islets neither the Greek radar, which was efficient, nor the Turkish, which was not, could spot them.

They were terrified of being caught by a real Turkish warship. The rotten old customs cruiser stationed in Bodrum had no radar and was usually broken down anyway. Like most seamen of the coast, Hamid hated and feared the Turkish authorities, and was almost friendly toward the Greeks. He knew, he said, that if they were caught by a Turkish patrol boat it was perfectly possible that they would be sunk on sight and left to drown. (This actually happened four years later to a Greek from Kalymnos, in the Karabaglar Islands. There was only one survivor.) The Greeks, on the other hand, would either allow them to surrender or pick them up after sinking them.

Hamid got one gold pound per oka, the old Greek measure which is about 2 ¾ pounds, for the first-grade Bodrum sponges, about half the going price in Europe, but worth taking to avoid the incredible complications of the Turkish customs and delays in payment due to transfers of exchange through the bank. In any case, said Kemal, "Why take this, when you can have that?" In one hand he waved a shaggy Turkish pound, worth at the time about thirty cents on the official exchange and less than five cents on the free market, and with the other he fondled a ruddy English gold sovereign.

"Those last forever," said Hamid.

Hamid was a student of scrap, and was very pleased by the kindness of the Romans in providing their ships with lead anchor stocks. Hamid was why we had never found and never would find a Roman lead anchor. He had salvaged and melted them down years ago. Kemal had also taken his share of sixteenth-century bronze cannons and lead anchors, but did not tantalize me with stories about things melted down for scrap. Hamid took positive joy in this.

"A lovely piece of lead. It weighed over a ton. It had writing on it, too, *roumi* [Greek] writing. Lead was high that year; I got a good price for it."

I was surprised when Kemal remarked that Hamid and Kiasim were experienced mine-disposal experts, indeed the best on the coast since the master mine-disposal man, their teacher who had learned in the Turkish navy, had disappeared at sea while on a diving expedition to the north.

"Probably shot up by the damned Greeks," said Kemal.

Hamid had made a lot of money from mines, for the explosive was live after it dried out and brought a good price from dynamite fishermen. I was impressed. Disarming mines is not for the unskilled or the fainthearted. There was evidently more to Hamid than met the eye, and although I knew that Kiasim was a master tinkerer and improviser, I had never suspected him of the specialized knowledge necessary for deactivating mines.

I asked Hamid how he went about disarming the big-gest ones, the ones that Kemal said were best because they yielded several dinghyloads of explosive.

"Do you mean the great big ones, like two oil drums put together?"

Evidently he meant German magnetic mines. These are booby-trapped from end to end, set to go off if you move them or if the hydrostatic pressure changes. They contain much more high explosive than bears thinking about.

"Well, do you know the door?"

I did indeed. It had at least two booby traps behind it, one mechanical and the other electrical, and some-times a third set to go when the lid was actually re-moved.

"I take a chisel and big hammer and knock off the nuts. Then I pry it off with a crowbar."

I asked if there were ever anything else that made it difficult to get the door open. Hamid gave me a conspir-atorial wink and grinned. We experts.

"Just the wires. I never worry about them, just rip 'em off . . ."

I subsided. As the divers say, God is big. It seemed unfair of Kemal to blame the Greeks for the disap-pearance of the man who had taught them to disarm mines.

We met Captain Ahmet Erbil, the man who discov-ered the Demeter bronze off Arap Adasi. He told us that when it had come up in the trawl he had decided to heave it back, but one of his sailors, an obstreperous type, had said, "Let's throw this crap back in the sea." So he had countermanded the order, to teach the crew that de-cisions were to be made by him, the captain.

They found the Demeter covered with sea growth, except for part of the face. They had thrown it on the beach, intending to cut it up for scrap, but it was confiscated by the government. As a reward they had received the equivalent of ten American dollars, less than the scrap value by weight of the metal. The cash value of the statue on the world market today would be not less than fifteen thousand dollars, a value difficult to fix because there have been so few genuine fourth-century bronzes put up for sale.

Uncle Ali — Infidel Ali, he was called — was the man who had put wheels on the *kangawa*, the sponge drag, in order to increase its efficiency. He spoke Greek and Italian as well as Turkish, but was strangely discreet about things he had found in the sea. Mad Ibrahim was also suspicious, but told us a little of sites we had mostly heard about from Kemal or his men. We tried to explain to them the interest of the past, why things dragged from or seen in the sea had a value, that the rotten wood fragments and broken pots told a story, and that the story was what was of value, not the pot.

For all the wrecks we had found, we had not yet seen anything that could make the archaeologists take notice. There were dozens of known wrecks of amphora carriers in the Mediterranean. No one was going to get excited about a few dozen more in Turkey.

We "found" the wreck we hoped for the night that an old captain from Istanbul, with whom Kemal had worked years before on a salvage job in the Bosporus, passed through Bodrum. Although they were now social equals, Kemal treated the old man with great respect. He was a master diver, he had been forty when Kemal was twenty, and he knew more than all of us combined.

The conversation turned to dynamite. We had all worked with it, and all began asking the old man what he would have done under this or that circumstance. We had a long discussion of the art of removing bronze propellers from wrecks that you have no right to salvage, how to dynamite a wreck so as to get at her copper boiler tubes, and how to cut up a wreck for scrap. I was fairly dazed by the time Kemal got around to what he had probably intended to ask the old captain in the first place.

"How would one go about dynamiting a mass of stuff grown flat onto the bottom, so that you could not get under it to break it loose?" he asked. He went on to say that the ingots were bronze, flat, and badly corroded. I did not pay much attention. He was probably talking about a cargo of mill ingot that went down in the nineteenth century.

It was very late when we staggered off to bed. I woke before dawn, with a dry mouth and a headache. I lay waiting for first light, when "the black thread can be distinguished from the white," and the muezzin's call would ring through the village to remind the people that prayer was better than sleep. I thought about our talk of the evening before, of dynamite and amatol and plastic, and the yellow metals that wait, intact forever, in the ruins of steel ships that rot away around them. I remembered how I once searched for and found the wreck of a steel ship in Hawaii. The hull had disappeared completely in seventy years, leaving only bits of the heaviest parts of the engines. When we raised the bronze propeller and hammered off the coral, the metal shone like new.

Like new.

But Kemal had said that the ingots were rotten. *Rotten?* Bronze ingots under the sea? But even bronze from Roman ships was often in pretty good shape. And where had I seen flat metal ingots before?

I got up, pulled on my bluejeans and shirt, and went to my packing box "library." There was a book there about the Minoans, and there was a reproduction of a painting at Thebes in the tomb of Rekme-Re, an Egyptian official who had died in the second millenium before Christ. It showed men with kilts and odd hair styles, naked from the waist up, bringing bulls' heads and jars and things that looked like giant flat dog biscuits to pile in a heap, while a disinterested Egyptian official looked on.

The book said that these men were "the men of Keftiu and the isles of the sea" mentioned by the Egyptians, and that the dog biscuits were copper ingots.

"Old rotten metal." "Men of Keftiu and the isles of the sea." "Minos expelled the Carians from the Islands . . ." These phrases stayed with me all day. That evening Mustafa and I ran into Uncle Mehmet. Did he remember the ingots that Kemal had told us about? Yes, indeed. Mehmet had been the diver who had first found the "bronze" under the sea. I asked if they had taken anything from the site.

"Bronze knives and a hatchet of bronze, not strong, because I took a piece of it home and it broke when the children played with it. There was a copper box too, full of black stuff . . ."

That night we asked Kemal about it. He did not want to talk. Mustafa thought that it probably was not important. I sensed that it was, but that it would have to wait. The next time that Kemal was feeling cheerful, after the new crankshaft had arrived from Izmir and had been installed, I asked him again. Both he and Mustafa insisted that it was not interesting and that it did not matter. I was increasingly convinced that it did matter, as I heard more about the place from Kiasim and Uncle Mehmet. Everyone got sick of my questions about the bronze pieces and finally Kemal, to make an end to the tiresome subject, promised that he would give me some pieces of metal when he dynamited the site for scrap.

On impulse, for I had no idea where I would get the money, I promised him that I would see that he got double the value of the scrap metal if he would hold off dynamiting the place until I had seen it, if I then decided to salve it myself. He agreed. The metal was rotten anyhow, which reduced its scrap value, and we were friends.

That evening I wrote in the dog-eared notebook:

The Bronze Ship

Located in the Gulf of Finike off Anadolu Burun. Lies off the point of the third small island off Finike, fifteen miles from Finike in the direction of Antalya where there is a group of six small islands. Depth is sixteen fathoms, bottom is rocky. This site was discovered by Kemal Aras, four years ago. He took a bronze spear from this place, which he remembers was very corroded, and at the same time brought up a small bronze box, from his description about the same size as two cigar boxes together. This he broke open and threw away when it proved to be empty. One of Kemal's divers remembers that the box was enamelled (*sic*) inside. Captain Kemal and two other divers, who were on board at the time, remember the place as follows:

Lying in a hollow of the rocky bottom on a shallow sand bar were six or eight pieces of bronze, each one about two metres long by three centimetres square (i.e. thick). There are also other bronze objects, so old and deformed that you cannot tell what they are. The whole mass is so stuck together that it cannot be moved.

Captain Kemal had planned to dynamite the place in the spring of 1959, but was dissuaded and agreed to show us the place instead. If this site is not investigated and protected within the next year, we feel certain that it will be dynamited and looted and that whatever remains there will certainly be sold for scrap and lost.

We are convinced of the reliability of the above information and feel that this site must be investigated in 1959.

The bronze wreck stayed in my mind all summer. I knew that Mehmet and Kemal had found something important. If there were bronze knives in the wreck, it had to be very old, before 1000 B.C. In all the reports I had read of the wrecks that had been found to date, none mentioned bronze knives.

Getting to Anadolu Burun was another question, as was finding the site after we arrived. Kemal was convinced that we would never find the place without him, and he was not going to be working down that way for another year. Even locating the place on a chart was difficult, because Kemal's name for the place was not the one given on the nautical charts, and we had no chart of the region which showed enough detail for us to describe the place so thoroughly that Kemal, who could not read charts, could recognize it. The place was 185 miles away, coasting, and the trip would not take less than a week or ten days, if we had a seaworthy boat, which we didn't. It was impossible by road. There were no roads to the area of the cape itself, and the nearest town, Finike, was twenty miles away from the islands.

Mustafa had a great deal of work to do in Izmir, and could not spare the time. A lone foreigner hiring boats and diving would attract unwelcome official attention. I was able to dive from Kemal's boat under the aegis of Kemal and Mustafa, but had no illusions about what would happen if I were to attract the attention of the authorities outside of Bodrum. Worst of all, we were nearly out of money. There was enough to finish the season in Bodrum, and that was all.

Finally, who really knew what was there? All the hard facts that I could get from Kemal and Mehmet were in the notebook, and while the information was convincing, I had heard other convincing stories that proved to be inaccurate or exaggerated when investigated.

Along with a dozen other sites that might be interesting "someday," the bronze wreck location went into the file and was put aside for the more immediate interest of the two complete wrecks at Yassi Ada, and the incredible mass of material that lay on the west reef there.

X

~~~~~

Yassi Ada II

RASIM HAD two weeks' leave, and Mustafa, after long
negotiations, had managed to borrow the only Rol-
lei Marine underwater camera housing in Turkey. The
plastic case that I had bought in Italy was broken and
could not be repaired because plexiglass cement did not
exist in Turkey.

Mustafa and Rasim's wives arrived from Izmir on the
bus, anticipating days on the beach acquiring sun tans
and cooking us good meals. Kemal would take us to the
islands and loan us the dinghy. We had food and water
for a week, after which *Mandalinche* would pick us up
again.

We set up camp on the little beach, excited by our first
chance to explore the island systematically and to get a
really good idea of what lay under the reef, under the
mud at Wreck III and at the other wreck which lay
nearby. By the end of the first diving day on the west
reef, we had found five new wrecks, all in the shallow
water around it. These were not much to look at, only
masses of broken shards from identical jars in heaps,
with scatterings in the direction of the big waves. When

pottery was shallower than twenty feet, it had almost always been smashed by wave action. Deeper, it was better preserved. At sixty feet most of the amphoras were in one piece.

I followed the scattered broken jars from the top of the reef, south from Wreck I into deeper water, and fetched up in the weed-grown area that we called the "end" of the wreck. Something about the weeds seemed strange, and when I parted them I discovered that there was another heap of first-century jars, all that was left of a ship. They were still stacked as they had been when she sank.

The jars were slim Rhodians with hooked handles, like the ones on the reef one hundred yards above, but when we raised one a day or two later, we saw that the clay was pink, not baked or mixed as well as the "genuine" Rhodians of the west reef, and the shapes were subtly different. Were these imitations of Rhodian jars? Was some trader taking advantage of a market for Rhodian wine to fake the "brand" shape of the Rhodian jars in order to sell an inferior product? The question has not been answered.

When the *meltem* stopped, the heat was grim. There was no shade, and the iron rocks threw out blasts of reflected sunlight. The tarpaulin that we rigged for the women failed to keep out the heat of the sun; with no wind, the patch of shade under it was a furnace. The beach was impossible to walk on with bare feet. Tools left in the sun soon became too hot to handle.

In the evening a tiny breeze sprang up, and the patch of beach cooled off. By the time we began our fine dinner of fried fish and tomato salad, prepared by the wives, we had forgotten the miseries of the sweltering day. The wind fell and the moon rose, showing the shapes of the islands like dark paper cutouts against the evening sky. A caïque without lights chugged by. Was it Hamid, on some illicit errand? Or a Greek trawler, poaching at risk of life and boat the almost unfished Turkish waters?

We drank a last coffee around the embers of the fire, and went to bed. I spread my blankets on the beach and the husbands and wives slept in the tent, which not long afterwards began to pullulate with screams from the ladies. Swarms of rats danced and chittered beside the embers of the campfire, and galloped in circles around the tent where the women curled in a ball, squealing. Rasim and Mustafa ran around blocking gaps in the tent where rats could enter. The rock where we had piled the larder was swarming with rats. Rasim and I waded waist-deep into the sea with our food stores and heaped them on another rock.

I dried myself and went to bed, wondering where in the world the rats had come from, as tiny feet pattered creepily over my blankets. There is no water except rainwater at Yassi Ada, and it does not rain for six or seven months a year, so that one assumes that trapped rainwater would have evaporated in the heat by the end of the summer. How then did those rats live? On the occasional dead fish washed ashore? On the tufts of grass that struggled fitfully for life in the crevices in the rocks where blown dust had collected and made a little soil? Years later, we asked a rat expert, and were told that rats need water at least once in twenty-four hours, and that the existence of rats on a waterless and unhabited island far from land was impossible.

The next morning the women mutinied. The sun was

too hot for sunbathing, and the rats were too much to bear. At length the women were persuaded to stay another day or two.

We set about further exploration of Wreck III, the globe-amphora wreck. We wasted two dives in finding the site again. Finally, we got our buoy anchored on one side of the wreck. The site measured about sixty feet long by twenty wide. At the upper end was a heap of anchors, each longer than a diver extended, and big around as a man's wrist. The metal was covered with sea growth which could not be scraped off. I broke off a piece. It was iron, or what was left of it, for the metal had turned into a black mush, its shape preserved only by the layer of concretion that had formed around it.

Searching in the sand beside the mass of round amphoras, we found bits of wood, part of heavy timbers which ran along the line of the edge of the amphoras. This was exciting, for it proved that some part at least of the hull of the ship was preserved under the muddy sand. We found the area of the cabin-galley, clearly distinguishable because of roof tiles and different types of pottery scattered in a ten-foot-square area. We brought up samples of every kind of pottery we found: bowls, small jars, and the two types of jars in the main cargo. We were very careful not to disturb the galley area or to dig too deep, because this was a shipwreck of a period never before investigated, the time of the beginning of the Byzantine Empire. The Yassi Ada ship, if properly excavated, could be the link between modern Aegean ships and the ships of ancient times.

For the first time we had a camera with a flash that would take color pictures. Rasim posed behind the anchors. The flash bulb went off perfectly. I reached for the bulb to remove it, and there was a tremendous bang. The reflector shot off the end of the flash arm and fell slowly to the bottom. It was settling between two of the big amphoras before I felt the shock in my hand. I saw that it was streaming with bright green blood. At that depth there were no longer any red rays in the light that came from the surface.

I managed to unscrew the jagged stump of the broken bulb, and got another bulb into the socket after refitting the reflector. I aimed at Rasim as he was swimming over the wreck, and had to move because the water was dirty. Supposing that I had kicked the bottom acciden- tally, I moved away. The dirt cloud stayed with me. Then I realized that I was swimming in a cloud of my own blood. I held my hand up, so that the blood streamed off to one side, and shot. The flash failed. My air came hard. The dive was over. My streaming hand reminded me of the deceptive presence of pressure at a hundred and twenty feet, strong enough to implode the bulb. It was over a year before I could feel anything with the thumb and palm of my right hand.

Kemal turned up before dark. We tore down the camp on the little beach, got everything on board *Man- dalinche*, and ran across the channel to Marilyn Monroe, big Karabaglar, where we camped. There were no rats.

That night I nearly went mad trying to understand Kemal's stories about diving to the wrecks of the Otto- man fleet that had been sunk by the Russians at Cesme, south of Izmir, in 1770. I could, with Mustafa's help, understand Kemal's stories when only Mustafa and I were the audience, but with Rasim and Mustafa together it was almost impossible to get Kemal to slow down so I could catch points that I had missed.

One day I experienced my only shark attack in five years of diving in the Aegean. I had been photographing a new wreck on the north side of Yassi Ada, one of the broken ones that consisted of nothing but smashed amphoras. I sensed something, and looked up to see a ten-foot blue shark charging me at what seemed to be full speed. Trembling with terror, I nerved myself to follow standard procedure and rushed toward him. He stopped, turned with a flash of his great tail, and swam swiftly away. I headed toward the shore and felt better with the rocks at my back. I thought I saw him once again, with two others, circling just outside my range of vision, before Mustafa, who had seen fins on the surface, came to get me in the dinghy. I was badly frightened. But was it really an attack, or was the shark simply curious?

It is certain that sharks are dangerous. A big shark of one of the aggressive species can swim twenty knots and cut you in two with one grind of his loose-socketed jaw. Still, there are few attacks in the Mediterranean, and in the folklore of Aegean sponge divers there are only a few stories, told by all the divers. One concerns the helmet diver on a Greek sponge boat off Crete. He surfaced far from the boat, and was cut in two by a big shark which struck from underneath.

There is a fantastic true story of a Kalymniote naked diver named Latari who dived into the mouth of a large shark, which he mistook for a sponge-bearing rock. He was holding the thirty-pound marble descending weight ahead of him. When the marble hit the pit of the shark's stomach, and Latari's waist was at tooth level, the shark regurgitated and threw out both Latari and the stone. Latari lived until the 1930's, and bore the great scars till he died.

Kemal and his men claim that air bubbles scare sharks away, but they are terrified of sea turtles which, they say, eat air hoses. But it is certainly true that Mediterranean sharks will take divers. In 1962, a porbeagle shark attacked a diver in Italy, who did not survive.

It seems that although there are few sharks in the Aegean, they are apt to be dangerous when they do appear. I have always resembled a spinning top when hanging on the decompression stage ever since that incident. They may be afraid of my air bubbles, but again they may not.

XI

~~~~~

The Cochran Expedition

I RETURNED to America in December, full of enthusiasm. This was the first time that a sponge captain had shown shipwreck sites to outsiders able both to understand and to visit them. We had doubled the known sites in the Mediterranean.

But editors were tired of pictures of broken pots with fish swimming around them, and professional archaeologist were weary of eager young men with tales of undersea wonders. Undersea archaeology was the realm of adventurers and treasure hunters. When I told the editors of one national magazine about the bronze wreck, they said that it was of course interesting, but that since I was not an archaeologist, they would not feel justified . . . But if I found something really important, like a Spanish galleon, I should certainly let them know.

Professionally, I had gotten myself into an interesting corner. The work that I was turning out was too specialized to be of journalistic interest. The scholars knew me for a journalist, and that was academic doom. Almost everyone questioned my motives.

Miss Grace gave the situation the push that it needed.

Head of the fourth-century B.C. Demeter found by a Bodrum sponge diver in 1953. It was this find which aroused interest in Bodrum.

Throckmorton and the Bodrum Castle, constructed of stones, some with inscriptions, taken from the ruins of ancient Halicarnassus and from the Mausoleum.

Coolest place in Bodrum one hot afternoon.

Turkish villagers in the cafe in the place
where the Greeks used to live.

"Kemal fixed me with his
wild drinking eye."

Village boys, Bodrum.

Activity in Bodrum harbor.
Unloading new amphoras from a caïque.

Mandalinche at dawn. Diver coming aboard.

Mandalinche anchored off Bodrum, while the men change clothes to go ashore.

Dressing Mustafa Kapkin for a dive.

Captain Kemal Aras at
the tiller of *Mandalinche*.

"Uncle" Kiasim.

The old man from Bozburnu.

Tosun Sezen.

Berk.

Ship's boys having dinner after the others have finished.

Captain Kemal oiling the air compressor that feeds compressed air to the
helmet divers. It was built in England in 1899.

Kiasim and Ali.

(*Left*) Diver Mehmet, the ship's clock and the depth gauge in window.
Depth gauge shows 15 fathoms (or 90 feet).
(*Right*) Cleaning and packing sponges.

Captain Kemal on the dressing bench
tending the life life.

Sponge diving on the rocky bottom, clearly showing
the typical bent-forward posture of the diver
dragging a hose.

Sponge diver underwater. Note how the *apoche* is lashed to the diver's breastplate. This is the bag in which sponges are carried.

The sponge diver rising to the surface. He has balanced his weight so that he is only slightly negative. These few pounds of negative buoyancy can easily be pulled to the surface by the *kulaozeros* or tender.

Panoramic view of our first camp at Karabaglar. The small boats are smugglers from Gumushluk who rendezvous here with Greeks from Kalymnos.

In camp for the night. Mustafa Kapkin cooking dinner. *Mandalinche* in background.

Our first camp at Yassi Ada. When we ran out of water Rasim improvised a
sail and went out to get some in this small boat.

Kiasim rowing to *Mandalinche* with a load of brushwood for the galley fire.

Photo courtesy of Mustafa Kapk

(*Left*) Kemal at the upper wreck on Yassi Ada west reef. The top of the reef is covered with amphoras, mostly of the first century A.D., from Rhodes. The main stack shows clearly here. (*Right*) The shallow wreck at Yassi Ada. Throckmorton, with the aqualung, breaking loose samples from the pile of amphoras.

Cleaning amphoras. Throckmorton and Divanli.

Photo courtesy of Mustafa Kapk

Cleaning an amphora of the
first century B.C. from the west
reef at Yassi Ada.

John Carswell drawing the first jars from Yassi Ada.

Mandalinche at anchor
in the Keramic Gulf.

"The big fish
that nearly killed me."

Photo courtesy of Mustafa Kapkin

The globe amphora wreck (Wreck III) at Yassi Ada. Honor Frost diving. The wreck carried a cargo of about 2000 amphoras. It was sunk on a muddy bottom, and a great deal of the hull of the ship was preserved under the mud. When the wreck was excavated, it was dated to about 620 A.D. by gold coins, evidently part of the ship's pay chest, which were found in the ruins of the cabin.

Tile wreck in the Gulf of Keramus. Honor Frost making preliminary drawings. The wood of the hull has rotted away from the tiles, except where it
has been preserved under a heap of tiles.

Pottery found in the galley area of this wreck dates it to the mid-seventh
century A.D., and is identical to that found in the galley area of Wreck III
at Yassi Ada. This detail shows the tiles stacked still more or less in order.

Lutfi Gelil mooring atop the Gelidonya wreck.

The crew relaxes. Ship's boy Osman, Kemal, Captain Nazif.

Uncle Mehmet on the bronze wreck site at
Cape Gelidonya as it was found.

(*Left*) Methods of working underwater. Bass and Claude triangulating.
(*Right*) Diver in background puts a bronze ingot into the basket, while
Duthuit, foreground, chips at an ingot.

"It took two of us to handle the lifting basket under water."

Cutting out the hull lump on a day when the current was not running. Claude and Uncle Mehmet chiseling in the gully. Scuba diver holds the drill — helmeted diver swings the sledge.

Claude Duthuit breaking loose lumps on the platform. One small lifting basket is partly filled, the other floating upside down on its lanyard, with the big boulder and the gully in the background.

One diver holds the airlift so that it is well under control, the other
sweeps the sand carefully with his hand. The airlift is a gigantic
vacuum cleaner. It works on the principle that compressed air,
injected into the bottom of the rigid tube, rises with great force,
expanding, thus creating a suction at the working end.

Lutfi Gelil handling the small airlift.

Duthuit working in the cut, giving an idea of the
depth of the cuts made to free the hull lump.

Prying up the lump. Frederic Dumas and Claude Duthuit breaking loose a lump off the platform with hydraulic jack. The copper
ingots and bronze tools were so solidly stuck together by 3200 years
of sea growth that there was no danger of breaking them.

The hull lump.

The hull lump.
The piece of wood with
tag No. 77 was probably the
keel of the ship.

Filling the balloon.

The balloon rises.

The lump begins to rise.

Underwater filming at Cape Gelidonya.
Stanton Waterman taking moving pictures.

Claude Duthuit struggles with the sheet he is attempting to wrap
around the lump so that no object will drop off on its way to the
surface.

Campsite. Walter, George and Mehmet cleaning the lump.

Throckmorton in the pool used for
washing objects, cleaning a lump.

The longboat, loaded with
copper ingots, pushes off
to *Lutfi Gelil*.

Bass and Miss Taylor cleaning objects.

Throckmorton at work in camp.

Photo courtesy of Herb Greer

Throckmorton and Bass.

Photo courtesy of Herb Greer

The beach at Cape Gelidonya as we left it.

Lutfi Gelil leaving Gelidonya.

Mace head, before cleaning.

Mace head, after cleaning.

Bronze mirror.

Blanks for making tools.

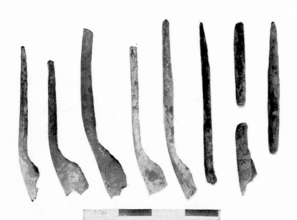

Bronze picks.

Shovel.

Double ax.

Hoes.

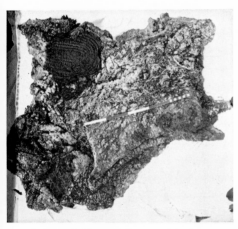

Lump with bronze ingot and basket.

Basket detail.

Ingot and pot.

Cleaned ingots.

Throckmorton
at work in Bodrum.

Knight's Hall
in the Bodrum Castle,
where the museum began.

On one of her periodic visits to Princeton, where she was a member of the Institute for Advanced Study, she chanced to meet Stan Waterman, who had made a career out of underwater filming and lecturing. He had been invited by a friend who had a large yacht to cruise the Aegean that summer. Stan came to see me with Drayton Cochran, owner of *Little Vigilant*, a steel-hulled, teak-decked motor sailer, ideal for our purpose with her luxurious quarters, generous deck space, freezer, and well-organized galley. I wrote Hakki Bey, who applied to his superiors in Ankara for funds and for leave to survey the coastal waters of southern Turkey for the Izmir museum.

Equipped with a portable decompression chamber, a big new Bauer air compressor that could fill tanks in twenty minutes instead of the two hours required by the battered wreck of the compressor I had brought from Italy the year before, and quantities of other gear, we sailed from Athens in the last week of June. We arrived to find that Hakki Bey's formal request for recognition and funds had been refused. Undaunted, he took his vacation. After all, the department could not tell him what to do in his free time, and there was no law forbidding us to dive in the sea. If we found any antiquities, his position as Director of Antiquities of the region allowed him to raise what he felt necessary for sampling purposes.

With Hakki Bey, his son Enis, Rasim, and Mustafa Kapkin, we sailed from Izmir for Bodrum during the first week of July. Besides my old friends from Izmir, our crew consisted of Stan Waterman; John Cochran, the captain's son; John Righter, a friend and sailing companion of John Cochran's; and Susan Phipps, John's fiancée. We dived all down the coast between Izmir and Bodrum, finding amphoras, and when we arrived in Bodrum we found that our sponge-diver friends had collected more in response to the appeal I had made the year before. Bodrum was full of amphoras, so full that space was becoming a problem.

Hakki Bey had a long talk with Osman Bey, the director of education in Bodrum, and received his permission to use the Knights' Hall of the Crusaders' castle as a storeroom. It was the only building in the castle that had a real door. Kemal dug around in his back yard, found a couple of amphoras, and hauled them up to the castle. In the Knights' Hall, plaster was peeling off the walls in sheets, and choking clouds of dust and dried mule dung rose when we scuffed our feet.

It didn't matter. It was a museum, and it was ours. The ruined walls grew in our imaginations, and we had visions of the stone-choked bailey as a park full of tourists in bright sport shirts, each of whom would contribute something to Bodrum's well-being.

Mustafa spent hours making sketch maps with Kemal, who would not be able to come with us, while I took copious notes. We hoped that by following his directions carefully we could find the bronze wreck. He doubted this. The bottom in that place was so broken up and rocky that even he would have a hard time finding it again.

At length we pulled out of Bodrum, heading south. It was strange to see the cliffs of Cape Krio, the blue outline of Symi spotted with white houses, and the long line of desert coves that led to Marmarice go by at twelve knots. I was used to seeing them in a blur of tooth-chattering vibration from *Mandalinche*'s deck. We stopped and dived along the way, finding other wrecks.

That evening we anchored in Finike harbor, near a launch which flew the American flag. She was a survey boat from the U.S.S. *Morey*, an American ship which was cruising the coast to make, after a hundred and fifty years, a survey which would replace the work done by Beaufort. The *Morey*, which anchored off Finike that evening, seemed with her wealth of modern technical equipment a very far cry from the H.M.S. *Frederick-steen*, thirty-two guns, which Beaufort had commanded. We visited the launch and ate monster steaks from their freezer. I remembered the fish and beans of *Mandalinche*, and thought of Cape Gelidonya, twenty miles away.

In the morning we headed for the barely visible blue cape. The three-hour run seemed longer. Halfway, two islands were visible. Kemal had said that there would be five. Beaufort remarked that Scylax, in his *periplus*, mentions only two, and two is all we saw as we came from Finike.

Looming up on the land side was Adrechan Cape, Strabo's Mount Phoenicus, now called Cape Gelidonya. It was flat calm, with no *meltem*. As we came closer, what had seemed two islands turned to three. There were faint specks of eagles circling over them. Five hundred yards off the nearest island Captain Cochran slowed the engines. Our wake crashed on the sheer sides of the nearest island, and washed into what must have been Beaufort's "deep cleft in the nearest of them [that] sheltered our boat from a heavy swell that rolled along the shore . . . its perpendicular sides screened the people while eating their dinner from the scorching rays of the sun. No trifling luxury, this, after the fatiguing operations of six hours, with the thermometer at 90 degrees in the shade."

It was already very hot, though not yet noon. The British sailors in their heavy clothing must indeed have been grateful for that deep cleft, when they ate their salt pork and hardtack there a hundred and fifty years ago.

Mustafa and I sighed with relief as the islands fell into place correctly according to the plan in the notebook. There was the third small island. There was the island shaped like a ship, and the big outer island. We ran in between them, over blue water.

There was a slight swell from the west, but no current. The place was not so bad, perhaps, as Kemal had painted it. Still, it was easy to see why Pliny had described it as "noxious to mariners." The sheer cliffs rose straight out of the water, with fangs of twisted volcanic stone protruding from them, ready to rip the guts out of a ship that touched them.

The captain hove to in the middle of the channel. Stan and I jumped over the side with masks and snorkels, to find the place where Kemal said a ridge ran under the water thirty feet down. The water below us was blue, and we could see no bottom. The burnt gray cliffs loomed over us. Stan shouted. He had spotted a ridge in the middle of the channel, where Kemal had said it would be. The captain ran over and anchored the ship on the spot. I swam down and found nothing but two small groupers in a cleft on the shallowest part of the rock.

After lunch we dived to search, spread out in a line with Mustafa leading. The bottom swarmed with fish. Fantastically broken up, it did not seem much as Kemal had described it. We finally came to a steep slope that went very deep, after seeing only a Roman cooking pot welded to the bottom by concretions, and a soggy Turkish newspaper.

Captain Cochran announced that we would leave the next day if we could not find the wreck. I was convinced that the Bronze Age ship was there, and so was Mustafa, but even Hakki Bey did not seem hopeful of our chances for finding it in the time available.

Morning broke clear and still, and the sea was like greasy bottle glass. We all went off in a line, following a compass heading to the island. At eighty feet we came to a huge rock. Mustafa and Stan Waterman went around one side, while I went round the other and was immediately lost. I wandered alone in a jungle of broken rock until my time was up.

Mustafa and Stan were waiting when I surfaced, having had a similar experience. There seemed little chance of finding the wreck in half an acre of boulders big as trolley buses. *Little Vigilant* trembled with the vibration of the engines warming up as we made one last descent. With Mustafa, I spent my diving time wandering aimlessly on the bottom in an impossible tangle of rock. I surfaced, hopeless.

When I reached the gangway, everyone was gathered around John Cochran and Susan Phipps. John held in his hand a heavily overgrown bronze double ax. He had decided to photograph Susan in a cave that we had passed the day before, and had seen the wreck on the way. Mustafa and Stan had been within a few feet of it the day before. Captain Cochran ran his ship around to anchor in the lee of the island.

When we steamed back into the channel next morning

we were greeted by a heavy swell, and the buoy marking the wreck was almost dragged under by the current. We hand-over-handed down the buoy line, holding our masks on our faces with our hands. The wreck lay at the foot of a slope, as Kemal had said, in a natural amphitheater of rock with a huge boulder at one end of it.

Almost invisible, dozens of copper ingots lay heaped on top of a rock that pushed out of the sand. They were stuck so solidly together that they could only be moved with crowbars. When we pried one off, we found a hollow under it, full of bits of wood preserved by the sand and by copper salts released by corrosion of the ingots. There were potsherds and bronze axes, adzes, and spear points. Most startling were bits of rope twisted out of reeds or grass. It was what seamen call fox lay, two strands of fiber twisted by hand.

It was an incredible coincidence that the wreck lay where it did. If it had sunk a few feet farther out, it would have fallen on sand and been covered forever. Higher on the rocky slope, it would have broken up completely and the pieces would have disappeared into clefts in the rock. As it was, just enough remained visible so that Uncle Mehmet had seen it.

The wind whipped around the sides of the island, swinging the ship on her single mooring. The current began to run faster, two knots, perhaps even three. We struggled to do our respective jobs. Mustafa made a sketch plan of the site, clinging to the bottom against the rush of water. I concentrated on taking photographs of the site.

There was not enough time. On the second day Mustafa surfaced feeling dizzy and sick. Fearing the bends, we watched him with apprehension for several hours.

That night the captain called a halt and we sailed for Rhodes. Mustafa was very ill, not normally seasick but dazed and retching desperately. When we changed watches at midnight he was vomiting blood. He felt better in the morning, and was altogether recovered when we reached the lee of Rhodes. There were no after-effects.

Sally Hinchcliffe, a young archaeologist friend of mine, was in Rhodes. She had spent the last several years sailing her very small boat around the Aegean, studying ancient trade routes. We dashed to the local archaeological library to look up our finds. I was as excited as I had been when I had first seen the ingots. What we learned was enough to tell me that my expectations of the year before had been justified. The wreck could definitely be dated to 1500 to 1000 B.C.

We scuttled between the library and the box on the ship's deck where the material we had recovered was stowed, examining objects and then returning to compare them with the books. We had to be careful, for if a knowledgeable local archaeologist had seen our discoveries, they might well have been confiscated and locked up. Honor Frost would then have no chance to draw them when she came to Bodrum, and with no proof of what lay off Cape Gelidonya, I could not hope to organize an expedition. There was no trouble. Captain Cochran sailed for Bodrum, to drop us off.

XII

~~~~~

Customs

AUGUST WAS a bad month. It began with the customs. Our portable air compressor had come into Turkey on my passport the year before, but when we had loaded our gear on board *Little Vigilant* in Izmir, Mustafa had listed it for customs so that we could remove it in Bodrum. The new director of customs in Bodrum, one of the boys from Istanbul with pointed shoes, noticed the old entry in my passport.

"Ah ha! This proves that you imported under false pretenses and illegally transferred the compressor to Mr. Mustafa, for see here, this is a declaration by Mr. Mustafa that the compressor belongs to him!" He somehow managed to look us both in the eye at once. "This is proof that you have committed a criminal offense. And now it is lunchtime. Good afternoon, gentlemen." He stood up and walked out of the office.

All the next day Mustafa argued with the customs man. Finally he accepted a bribe, our eating money for the next month. My cameras, the portable decompression chamber that I had bought from Cochran, and most of our diving equipment remained in customs and were doomed to stay there until we could pay an additional heavy bribe. When I left Turkey for good, over a year later, the chamber was still there.

That evening one of our friends in the village, an educated man, walked up to the castle with us. I saw that he was crying, put my arm around his shoulder, and then he began sobbing, beating his hands against the great stones of the castle keep.

"Goddamn Turkey, goddamn this dirty country! We are a dirty country!"

We no longer had any desire even to think. We went down to the dock, where we met Kemal. Mustafa told him what had happened, and we spent the evening discussing in detail what we would do with our friend, the customs man, if we had the power.

During the next month I dreamed several times each week about murdering the customs director. This dream usually came after I had wished him a polite good evening, as he promenaded up and down the pier, the new one built with American aid, wearing one of the new suits he had bought with my money.

This question of the customs, of incidents like ours with the compressor, was always the big problem of working in Turkey. In three years there, we spent more time arguing with the customs than we ever did in diving, or in any other activity.

Besides the customs there were also the police, the coast guard, the gendarmerie, the customs police, the army and navy, and last, but very far from least, the secret police. These organizations have to exist, for the same reasons that similar, if fewer, organizations exist in Europe and America. But in Turkey, where society tends to be insecure and corruption is a way of life, no one ever trusts anyone else. Many officials are bribable. Therefore the honest official tends to pass the buck, because if he allows anything that is remotely questionable, he can lose his job, condemned by his superiors for taking bribes (i.e., taking a bribe and not giving them their cut). The worst of it was that the Turks I knew were basically honest and honorable people who had the misfortune to live in a society where honesty, as a practical matter, was impossible.

I made friends with the Director of Education, Osman Bey, and the new local doctor. They set themselves to teach me grammatical Turkish, and I began to talk freely. Young Hassan, the six-year-old son of the keeper of the waterfront cafe behind which we lived that summer, became my disciple. He was proud to carry my spear gun to the breakwater. When I sat typing my notes, he would sit beside me, mouth agape with wonder at the little foreign letters appearing magically on the paper.

His father was very poor, sunk in the slothful despair which overtakes so many Turkish villagers. His cafe was in the best location in town, yet it was filthy. All he served was tea, and he did not often bother to serve that, because he was too lazy to light the fire. If you woke him from his doze he would just click his tongue and say "yok." Almost everything was "yok" with Hassan's father. Three times a day he went to the mosque. He dawdled around the cafe the rest of the time, and in the afternoon he slept. I never saw him move quickly, never saw him shaved, and never heard him answer in the affirmative to anything.

He became a symbol to me of the result of the official system in Turkey. Why bother? Why work hard, when you can't keep it? Allah provides: be thankful. Little towheaded Hassan, who looked like Huck Finn and was bursting with intelligent curiosity, never got enough to eat, nor did his ten or eleven living brothers and sisters. I wondered how long it would be before he lost his enthusiasm and settled into the attitudes that he would have to acquire in order to stay sane.

It was a strange world of Kafkaesque drama that we lived in that month. The simplest affairs were complicated. We spent our miserable days in the customs house. I grew irritable, and silly in my irritation. Mustafa took the brunt of my bad temper. My trouble was that I believed that all these difficulties could be solved reasonably. If my equipment was stuck in customs, there must be a correct way to get it out. I could not understand that the customs man had no intention of ever letting it out. Our application for permission to use the equipment had been submitted to higher authorities, who would in turn submit it to yet higher authorities, until someday, along with thousands of others, our petition would arrive on the desk of the person who would make the decision. When would it arrive? A year from now, two years, who knew? Why bother? The answer would inevitably be "yok."

A friend of mine who has spent most of his life in the Middle East once remarked, "They eat you, slowly and definitely they eat you." He meant that they waste your time and sap your spirit. We Westerners assume, almost instinctively, that laws have something to do with justice, that telephones will work, and that people know their jobs. The Bodrum villagers, and the officials with whom I was dealing, assumed the opposite, avoiding the frustration that maddened me.

The summer wind came off the plains of Anatolia, blowing up dust devils in the streets of Bodrum and driving everyone to cool shade by noon, when I went out onto the white glare of the breakwater to spearfish and revel in the cool water. The fish fed us or our friends, or were traded to the restaurant for meat.

Honor Frost, this time unaccompanied, arrived and went to work in the dusty museum, drawing the material from the bronze wreck. In spite of the customs man, things began to go better. I talked and talked, in the café, to anyone who would listen, saying that our work would benefit the town and that the museum would bring tourists when it was completed. The villagers began referring to it as "our" museum, and appeared with offerings for it: broken lamps, coins found in the garden, and the inevitable amphoras. Three of the village officials came separately to me and apologized for the customs man.

Because we were there, because anyone could visit us and see what we were doing, and because our sponge-diver friends told anyone who would listen true stories of our adventures together, it was hard for false rumors about us to originate. The general attitude was, among the divers, that we were colleagues doing a hard job. The other villagers might have thought we were mad to want to do what we were doing, but didn't seem to suspect us of anything more sinister. The price we paid for this acceptance was a total and absolute lack of privacy which was as unnerving as it was unavoidable.

Captain Kemal and I went to see his patron, Zeyat Mandalinche, in whose honor Kemal had named his sponge boat. Zeyat Bey, on vacation from Ankara, was the delegate to parliament for the district, and a power in the land. He was charming in French and English, and invited us to visit him at his summer home in Gumushluk, the coastal village nearest the Karabaglar Islands. Gumushluk had been a fair-sized town in classical times, and had been besieged by Alexander. Now almost nothing remained except the ruined houses of the Greeks, abandoned since the great exodus of 1922. A pretty chapel, converted into a barn, stood on a knoll.

Zeyat Bey suggested that I spear a fish for lunch. With his party following in a rowboat, we swam around the bay, over the well-cut Hellenistic stones of the ancient port, which like so many other waterfronts on the coast had sunk about six feet. At the north end of the bay, the broken stones of an ancient jetty tumbled to forty-five or fifty feet. There were groupers there, but they were wary. After a dozen deep dives I was exhausted, shivering, and fishless. The deputy and his friends got bored and rowed off to shore.

The frustrations of the past weeks rose in my mind, and all my anger centered on the task of spearing a fish. I had to get a fish; it was expected of me. I had overheard Kemel boasting of my prowess as a fisherman. I crawled exhausted to the beach, out of sight of everyone, and stretched out in the sun to rest and get back some of the warmth I had lost. In half an hour I felt better and, remembering the greenish stain that indicated a reef in the middle of the harbor, swam out to the place.

I approached very carefully and saw a lovely big grouper peeping up at me, just a shadow under the rock twenty feet below. I swam along till I was out of his line of sight, dived, and doubled back behind him. I picked my way silently with my hands over the rock, peered round it, saw the yellow underside of the big head still pointed toward where I had been, and shot him. I hugged him, got my fingers into his eyes, and swam exulting back to shore. He must have weighed twelve pounds.

Zeyat Bey became expansive over the luncheon table. We discussed southern Turkey and the missing Greeks, and how the coast was dying, for its bloodstream had been the Aegean. The Dodecanese islands and the coast had been an economic unit for 3000 years. After 1922 all trade between coast and islands had been cut off. In Gumushluk the only remaining activity was the cultivation of oranges, which Zeyat Bey was promoting as his father had done before him. This, said he, was why he had taken the name of Mandalinche, which means orange, when Kemal Ataturk decreed that all Turks should take last names.

Before we left I walked out to the point and watched the sun set behind the Karabaglar Islands, and Yassi Ada, where so many wrecks lay. On the way back to where our car waited, I noticed some steel scrap, evidently part of a ship, lying on the beach. I asked a villager what it was, and he replied that some Greeks had been wrecked there.

"Allah curse the Greeks and all pig-eaters," he added, spitting on the ground. He turned his back and walked away.

His rudeness concealed one of the heroic stories of the Second World War, and the ignoble part played in it by the villagers of Gumushluk. In September, 1943, three Allied destroyers were steaming southwards down the Chuka channel off Yassi Ada. Two were British. The third, though British-built, was manned by the Greek navy. A few weeks earlier the Germans had laid a new mine field and the patrol steamed into it at fifteen knots. One struck and sank with her screws still spinning. A second disappeared in a flash of cordite as her magazines went. When the spray settled, one ship was still afloat. It was the *Adreas*, flying the Greek flag. The mine had gone off under her Number Two gun mount, and set off her forward magazine. Forty feet of her bows were missing. The guns of the Number Two mount pointed straight up from where they had been flung, against the bridge. Her screws hung half out of the calm water, which rose to deck level forward. A third of her crew were dead or dying, trapped in the mangled wreckage of the forepart of the ship.

The watchers on the shore waited for her to sink. Miraculously, she floated. Her boiler-room bulkhead held, although spouting water from a hundred popped rivets and shrapnel holes. Her engineer reported to the captain, giving her an hour to live, and with blood and fuel oil staining the sea they steamed for the nearest beach, Gumushluk. They beached her inside the bay, on the smooth sand. There was no welding gear on board and some men died in the tangled wreckage.

The crew slept beside the rotting corpses until a salvage tug with welding equipment came from Istanbul and the bodies could be cut out and buried. They burned off the dangling plates and reinforced the bulkhead with concrete. The Turks wanted to impound the ship, since belligerents were allowed only forty-eight hours in a neutral port.

But one night two months later her crew eased the *Adreas* off the beach and steamed safely to Alexandria. The Turks were furious. Although the coastguardmen watching her were armed only with old Mauser rifles, no match for the *Adreas's* remaining guns, they were court-martialed and imprisoned. The people of Gumush-luk demonstrated their anger in another way. They dug up the bodies of the dead Greek sailors, and fed them to the village dogs.

XIII

~~~~~

Simşek

I WAS sitting in the "office" typing when small Hassan, the cafe keeper's son, dashed into the room. "The mayor wants you!"

I followed him up the main street to the park by the city hall, where a crowd had gathered around a huge and polished limousine. Osman Bey saw me and waved. Beside him I recognized the mayor, the chief of police, and Zeyat Bey, the deputy to parliament. There was yet another man whom I did not recognize. They were all dressed in suits with clean shirts and neckties, and I was suddenly and uncomfortably conscious of my oil-stained bluejeans and khaki shirt. I wished that I were wearing shoes. I approached, trying to act as if I belonged there.

Osman Bey stood beside the unidentified man, a very imposing gentleman who wore a beautifully cut woolen suit. "Your Excellency," he said, "I want you to meet Peter."

I struggled for my best brave, frank look, while His Excellency inspected me as if I had just crawled out of a drain. I murmured a silent prayer of thanks to whatever had inspired the barber to offer me a free haircut that morning, in return for the fish I had given him the week before.

"It's the Governor," whispered Zeyat Bey.

"We told him he must see our museum," added Osman Bey with a wink, and led the way up to the castle.

Luckily we had swept the Knights' Hall that morning, and damped the dust. Prompted by Zeyat Bey and Osman Bey, who helped me with my bad Turkish, I explained the collection of objects that Honor and I had arranged neatly in an alcove a few days before. The Governor, panting a little from the climb, listened without enthusiasm, then asked why I wanted to salvage things from the sea. I hesitated, trying to find a short sentence that would explain.

Osman Bey broke in to repeat a quotation that I had laboriously translated into Turkish for him the week before: "Those who do not remember the past are condemned to repeat it."

The Governor asked quietly what I expected to find in the sea. I replied that I didn't know until I'd found it. He laughed, and turned to look at a stack of broken amphoras. There was a chorus of explanation of what they said, according to the Big Broken Pot Lady of Athens, and the Governor, for a moment, caught some of the wonder of the lost ships.

Osman Bey began a vivid description of the museum as it would look someday, and how it would draw tourists, and how we would hang big underwater photographs of the wrecks on the walls. The great man asked how I took photographs underwater. Osman Bey helped me explain.

The Governor then asked to see an underwater camera. We explained that it was in customs, and walked in a body down the castle steps and into the customs house. There my cases of equipment were dragged out of a dusty locker and I extricated the underwater Leica housing that I had brought from America. After coffee at the customs house, the Governor's party climbed into the big car, leaving Osman Bey and me standing in front of the door with other minor retainers. Osman winked. Three days later the customs director sent for me. He had found, he said, a regulation that made it possible to release my cameras.

The money that Hakki Bey had promised for preliminary repairs to the castle came from Izmir. It amounted to the equivalent of only fifty dollars, but it came from the government, and it meant that the castle was now a protected archaeological site. We hired masons and repaired the breeches in the wall that had allowed people from the outer villages to use the keep as a latrine on market days. Uncle Ahmet, who had been guardian of the castle for forty years, appeared one day in a brandnew uniform cap.

The money did not go far. I went spear-fishing and we paid the men in fish. A man brought a sack of cement, as a gift for "our" museum, he said. One of Kemal's acquaintances had a truck. Captain Kemal and Kiasim got him drunk one night and he loaned it to us to haul stone. When the broken walls were patched, Uncle Ahmet inscribed a circle in the wet cement with a stick and scratched "Ahmet 1959." We had a museum.

Honor Frost finished drawing the copper ingots and bronze tools which had come from Cape Gelidonya. There was nothing more to do about the Gelidonya wreck until we could return with a proper expedition, with money and equipment for a real excavation.

Sleepy Hussein of the waterfront cafe had a friend, also named Hussein, who owned a twenty-five-foot launch called *Simşek*. The boat was incredibly dirty, with an unreliable engine, but cheap to rent. Kemal suggested that we act as *Mandalinche*'s depot boat. If we would carry her extra fuel and supplies, set up camp, and cook for *Mandalinche*'s crew, he would pay for our food and fuel. Honor, Mustafa, and I could have *Simsek* for ourselves most of each day, which would make it possible to survey sites without tying up *Mandalinche*.

Hussein tacked old tin cans over the worst gaps in *Simşek*'s planking, and we set off. The Keramic Gulf is ringed with mountains, tall pine trees, and sandy beaches where we could moor with stern anchors out and bows just touching the shore. Every night we feasted on fish and octopus caught that day, with red, red watermelon or oozing ripe figs for dessert. We saw beehives everywhere in hollowed-out logs, the ends plugged with cow dung. The bees swarmed like flies. In the twilight we had to be careful not to eat them with our dinner.

We stopped at Keramos, where Antony had visited Cleopatra. I went ashore to drink tea with the men in the little cafe. It was strange to sit inside a room after two weeks of being in the open and always on board a boat. The room rocked and the men's voices hummed. As everywhere on the coast, sodden, depressed-looking peasants sat and stared, but they were very friendly.

That evening the ship's boy, Samy, and I walked a mile up the road to ancient Keramos. The modern town huddled in the ruins, built from stones that once formed Greek temples, Roman triumphal arches, and city walls. Pieces of columns lay beside the roadway for the stone-breakers and the gravel on the road was marble recently broken. Samy and I marveled at the great architraves and columns and capitals scattered over the heaps of ruins. We passed a shy woman who was working in her field to the tune of a squeaky water wheel driven by a blind donkey, who told us to watch the dog, and offered us water to drink.

At dusk we walked through the fields past masses of indefinable ruins and dozens of stone sarcophagi, the tops of which had been broken open generations ago, and met a man named Barbarossa who insisted on taking us to his orchard to give us all the ripe figs we could carry.

We cruised the bay. When we met villagers, they were very simple and friendly. Our only danger was the coast guard, or the gendarmerie. Although we had papers, it was possible that we would be arrested if caught under circumstances which they considered suspicious. The bays were good shelter, as they had been for the British Commandos in the Second World War who smuggled arms and men into Greece in boats like *Mandalinche*. Like us, they had used the deserted coves of Keramos for shelter, as had the smugglers of Samos and Kalymnos, and generations of pirate rowing galleys.

If we had had a good day, Kemal would break out the raki and tell tales of the great days in Bodrum, when he and Kiasim and Devil had been the wildest bucks on the coast, with silk shirts on their backs and gold pounds in their pockets. I remember one story particularly. We had anchored in a little bay and dined on the beach under the bows of the boats. Kemal and Kiasim began to reminisce about the days of the *fernez*, when they all worked for Ali Effendi.

They had been diving off Çeşme. Kemal went over the side first that day. On the bottom in fifteen fathoms, he followed the shoreline, keeping the deep water on his right hand. When his time was almost up, he saw a big chain stretching seaward. He followed it.

Twenty years later, Captain Kemal sat at one end of the piece of old canvas that served us as a dinner table. It was spread with hardtack, a plate of sliced tomatoes, a small glass, a tin cup, and a bottle of Yeni raki, half full. When he stopped speaking the silence was broken only by the crash of small waves on the beach and the steady hiss of the kerosene lantern, which threw its hard glare on the impassive faces of the men sitting around the canvas.

Uncle Mehmet grinned in anticipation. The captain waved the tin cup toward the outer darkness. Samy appeared, took the cup, and went off with a crunch of bare feet on the gravel. In a moment he set the cup, dripping from the spring, before the captain, who tipped a little water into the raki in his glass, sipped, and looked up. His narrowed eyes moved from one man to the other.

"Its links were longer than my arm, and it ran along the sloping bottom, going deeper. I followed it until it began to rise up toward something like a cliff. When I got nearer, I saw . . ." — his voice rose and he leaned forward onto his knees. He pointed out into space, as if measuring height — "Wallah . . . a ship!!"

The whites of the men's eyes gleamed as they looked up. Like them, I could imagine the bulk of the wreck towering over us, half visible in the gray-blue water.

The lamp popped and the light flickered. Kemal sat back, reached for his glass, sipped, and handed it to Kiasim. Someone rose and pumped the lamp. The squeak was loud in the breathless silence. Kiasim sipped and passed the glass to Uncle Mehmet. The captain reached for a piece of bread, dipped it into the oil in the tomato plate, put it into his mouth and chewed slowly.

"I let air into the bag and rose, holding on to the chain, as far as the hawsepipe, which was so big I could have crawled into it. Then I jumped to the fo'c'sle railing. There was a big davit for lifting the anchor. I got hold of it with my right hand, settled myself, and looked aft.

"She lay upright. I could see as far as the bridge, which was on a level with the fo'c'sle because of the angle at which she lay, with her stern sloping down into deeper water. Her masts were still standing and the booms were rigged out as if to handle cargo. I heard a dull booming coming from way aft. I hesitated, then decided to go anyway. I let go the derrick, slid to the after fo'c'sle railing, climbed over, and jumped down onto her well deck by the Number One hatch. It was closed, with the covers still in place. I tried to move one of them, but they were held by iron straps.

"I slid aft until my hose and lifeline caught in the foremast shrouds. I was untangling myself when Ali started jerking for me to come up. I tied the lifeline on one of the winches for a marker, and floated up the mast. There were big *kapa* sponges growing there, one on the very top. I pulled it off and floated for a minute with my hand on the place where it had been. I felt like a bird, perched there on top of the mast. She seemed in as good order as one of those big ships we see alongside the dock in Izmir, except for the weed on her decks, the swung-out davits with the falls swaying in the current, and the fish swimming in and out the pilothouse windows."

[141]

The captain sighed, thinking of when he was eighteen and could go, naked, twenty-five fathoms in a *fernez* rig. The men sighed with him, thinking of the wealth in that virgin wreck. Lead. Brass. Bronze. Copper, worth two days' wages a kilo. Mysterious cargo under those closed hatches and perhaps gold, gleaming yellow in the purser's safe, untouched by time, corruption, and sea rot.

"We put the rig on Bayram, the first diver. Ali himself took the lifeline and gave Kiasim the hose. We watched the gauge go to twenty-three fathoms, the depth of the winch where I had tied the lifeline. When it dropped to twenty-five and then twenty-eight, we knew that Bayram was exploring the after end of the ship. The gauge went back to twenty-five, and he signaled for more hose. I imagined him in the saloon, and felt angry that I had missed first grab by finding the wreck so late in the dive.

"After twenty minutes Ali Kaptan signaled Bayram to come up. No answer. He tried again. Bayram answered, and the hose went slack. The gauge went to eighteen fathoms. Bayram signaled for more hose. The gauge went to fourteen, and stuck. Bayram asked for still more hose. We gave it out, and waited. Ali Kaptan tried to signal again. No answer. The line felt dead. The gauge still read fourteen fathoms. It was stuck, like the lifeline. Ali Kaptan held the lifeline between two fingers, to feel the least pull. The man at the tiller let the boat fall off a little too much and Ali cursed him."

Kemal drank half the milky mixture in the little glass and handed it to Kiasim, who knocked the rest back with a gulp, winked at Kemal, and put the glass down. Kiasim rummaged in the pocket of his stained canvas shirt. He pulled out a pack of Bafras, extracted three, handed me one and flipped the other to Uncle Mehmet.

When he got his cigarette lit, he took a big drag and said, "He was a diver, all right, a diver."

Kemal began to guffaw, gestured toward the rising moon, and said, "Wallah, that Bayram, he was a diver! Why, Mehmet here remembers the time that he and Ab-I-Din . . ."

I interrupted to ask, "What about the wreck, Kemal Bey?" The men looked at me gratefully. They wanted to hear the end of the story too, but didn't dare interrupt.

"Ah ha!" Captain Kemal fixed me with his wild drinking eye, and the men froze to attention. We all imagined the deck of that boat, rolling in the glassy September sea so long ago.

"Didn't I tell you he was a diver? We were already thinking about where to bury him when he popped out of the water on the far side of the boat and yelled at us. We pulled him aboard. He was fine, except for a little blood coming out of his mouth. We wrapped him in a blanket and sat him in the bows. Old Ali gave him a slug of raki, and when he got his breath, he began to talk.

" 'You put the line on the winch,' Bayram said. 'When I got as far as the masthead, I saw that the shrouds would foul my lines if I went that way, so I went down them to the bulwark, along the deck past the second hatch. There was a way under the bridge, all open at one side, with cabins on the other. I passed the place where they cooked. There were pots still in the racks, and a big stove with coal still in it. Instead of a fire there was a grouper in the oven, with his head sticking out, looking at me!

" 'I went aft, looking in at the portholes, but it was

dark inside and I couldn't see. I heard a booming sound and turned back to the place where they had the *gasinosu*. The door was open, and I went right in. It was light inside, because there were big windows. There were tables all around, in place, but the chairs were all in a heap in the corner. Lots of unbroken plates were in racks and scattered over the deck. I took some of them, and put them in my bag. I saw something move and was afraid, but it was only a curtain swaying in the current. I touched it and it fell apart. In the after end of the room there was a door ajar. I pushed it but it stuck, so I squeezed by into a long dim passage. It was hard to walk because of the slope of the deck.

" 'Then I heard the booming again, and saw something move in the end of the passage. It was bigger than me. I tried to go through the door again and got caught. I tried to get free. Something ripped and I fell down. Everything went black. I was afraid until I understood that it was only the mud that I'd raised by falling. I saw the light of the door and managed to get through it, with the big thing still at the end of the passage, moving toward me slowly.

" 'I got out into the big room, and whatever it was didn't follow. I filled the bag with plates, lots of good plates of all sizes. Then I went out the way I came. I thought of having a look at the captain's place, so I made myself light and climbed up the ladder onto the boat deck. I was just looking in when I got the signal. I went up, but the hose was caught around a davit. I tried to keep the plates and get back to the davit. I did, but I couldn't get the hose off because it was wrapped around the boat fall and I had no knife.

" 'So I left the plates by the davit, with the weights, went as high as I could, and came up free.' "

Kiasim grinned at me and said, "Didn't I tell you he was a diver?"

All the men relaxed and Kemal signaled for the bottle, and the ceremony of pouring drinks was repeated. Before Kemal and Kiasim could change the subject, I asked what finally happened. They told me the rest of the story in a rush.

They had buoyed the hose and cut it loose, and had dived with another rig to clear it. The hose came up with the weights and the sack full of plates attached to it. The plates were beautiful, white with a blue crest and pictures on them. Bayram began to brag about how they would look in his house. Ali Kaptan said that they belonged to him, and there was a big argument. Finally, in a rage, Ali Kaptan threw the whole lot overboard, saying it was their business to pick sponges, not salvage junk.

The war came, and they never went back. "She's still there, Peter," said Kemal. "Maybe we'll go back someday. No one knows where she is but Kiasim and me. The others who were on that boat are all dead."

I went to bed thinking about that virgin wreck, wondering what Bayram had seen in that dark passage. I remembered the worst scare that I'd ever had diving, when I was in a new wreck, sixty feet deep, in a pitch-dark passage. Something threw its arms around me and squeezed. I was paralyzed with terror until I realized that it was a mattress.

We worked our way around the gulf and dived on several very interesting wrecks. One was the ship loaded with tiles which Devil had told us about. The tiles, tons of them, were piled as they had fallen when the hull rotted out from under them. As Devil had said, they were as big as washboards. They were marked with double vees on their inner sides, potters' marks scratched in the wet clay nearly fifteen hundred years before. In the galley area, we found amphoras and cooking pots like the ones from the globe-amphora wreck.

I lost a chance for a marvelous photograph because the flash failed to work. It had been locked in customs and I had been unable to check it. That same afternoon I spent three hours checking the circuits of the flash and overhauling the wiring. I tested it with three precious bulbs and it worked perfectly, but the next day underwater it failed again. The battery was evidently too weak, and there was no possibility of getting another in Turkey. Knowing this, I had long since ordered a replacement shipment, but this too was naturally held up by customs.

I was enraged by the hopeless frustration of the whole situation. Not only had I lost one really good picture, but also a week of interesting and important color photography. Customs regulations normally exist to protect the economy of a country, but the Turkish customs situation seemed to have a life of its own, having nothing to do with me, my equipment, or any Turks I ever met. It was a hopeless mess, which stopped or impeded every step we tried to make.

Mustafa couldn't spend any more time away from his job, so he reluctantly resigned and returned to Izmir. Both he and I were afraid that I wouldn't be able to deal with the people without him.

Honor and I went back to Yassi Ada with Hussein

and "Captain" Ibrahim in *Simşek*. We got along very well, and I found that I could talk freely to both Hussein and Ibrahim without trouble. We worked for a week more, and by the end of it had a fair idea of what the globe-amphora wreck was like. The metal pieces we now knew to be definitely anchors, corroded so that the metal was like mush, but with the shape preserved by the rough coating of sea growth that had formed around them before the iron had gone. These must have been lashed together on the ship's port fo'c'sle.

The material we raised from the "galley area," the patch in the middle of the after end of the heap of jars, hinted at the exciting discoveries that George Bass and his team would make several years later on the same site.* We found part of a copper tray, several cooking pots, and two kinds of tiles. When Bass excavated the wreck, the cabin area was to yield a wonderful cross section of material, including a steelyard with the captain's name on it. But that is George Bass's story. We left the wreck with a rough sketch plan in hand, and the information that would make planning a future serious excavation possible.

Honor went back to England, and I made short trips with Kemal, spending half my days in Bodrum. It was fall. The wind from the north was more brusque, and cooler, though the land wind was still hot and dry. The district had been more than half a year without rain. We were always tired, and at evening the skin felt tight over our cheekbones. Kemal said that it was the dive fatigue that all sponge divers had at that time of year.

* "Underwater Excavations at Yassi Ada: A Byzantine Shipwreck," *Archäologischer Anzeiger*, 1962.

George Bass, *National Geographic Magazine*, Vol. 124, No. 1, July, 1963.

The month before I had been full of bile, western European Calvinistic bile. I had been impatient and often unhappy because someone was not doing what he was supposed to do, or what I wanted him to do. Now I was almost as patient as they. Anger, an unnecessary emotion, came hard. I began to find that quality the Turks call *kayf*.

My change in attitude was brought home one morning when I was in Hussein's cafe, drinking tea and talking to crazy Captain Mustafa, the old pirate who ran the boat to Kos. The policeman appeared with some German tourists, two men and a middle-aged woman. They spoke good English. I have no idea who they thought I was, since I wore bluejeans and a sponge diver's denim shirt, and had not recently shaved.

They wanted to visit the castle. I sent little Hassan off to get the guardian, and settled down to talk. It was pleasant to speak my own language. Half an hour passed. I was glad for the excuse not to have to go to work, and happy to be making a show of hospitality. The woman asked when the watchman would come.

"Soon," I said.

"But when is soon?" she asked.

Like a Turk, I answered, "Allah knows."

She stood up angrily and announced that she was bound for Ephesus and refused to be delayed any longer.

"Don't worry," I answered her. "Wait, and he will come."

She replied that the waiting bothered her, although it did not seem to bother me. If, said she, I hadn't become "Turkized," I would understand her point of view. What fools, I thought as they marched off without saying good-by, and then realized that I might well have done the same a year before.

I decided to go to Kos, the island the Knights of St. John had called Stanko. Apparently some Crusader had asked a Greek where he was going, and the Greek had replied, "Stin [to] Kos," which the Crusaders had then corrupted to Stanko. The Turkish name is Istankoy. All of which illustrates the misunderstandings which arise from imperfect understanding of a language.

I anticipated a few days' respite from the continual strain of speaking Turkish, and looked forward to talking to someone new, a foreigner or an intelligent Greek. I was weary of the same conversations every day. My worst hardship in Bodrum, total lack of privacy, was nerve-racking in the extreme, and the state of mind engendered by it was dangerous, because people in Bodrum were most often friendly and meant well. There were just too many of them. Someone new was always appearing to ask the eternal questions: where was I from, how old was I, was I married, was my father living, did I expect to find gold, and was I afraid of sharks? It was hard to be consistently polite and responsive.

I set out for Kos, looking forward to a room by myself, a shower, a meal all alone in a shady cafe, perhaps even reading a magazine. The greatest luxury of all was the idea of seeing women. The strange life I had been leading in Bodrum started me thinking about the whole question of the Turks' attitude toward women and, in a way, my own. At the moment women were more important symbolically than as actual sexual objects. I was not interested in women physically when I was diving, for like most divers, I was always tired. What bothered me in Bodrum was the absence of the idea of women as possible companions. I was not demoralized so much by the absence of women as by the suspicion that nubile women didn't really exist at all. I wanted to sit and watch the pretty girls of Kos walk by, not necessarily even speaking to them, but simply renewing my imagination with the assurance that pretty girls actually existed in the world, wearing nice clothes so that men would look at them.

We chugged into the harbor on the rotten old wreck that served as the twice weekly ferryboat, and I was struck by the beauty of the little ships in Kos harbor. The caïques of Kos, like the women, were well painted and kept with pride, unlike the shabby ships of Bodrum. But there was no hotel space in Kos and I had to accept the captain's invitation to sleep on the dirty caïque with the rest of the men from Bodrum. I was stuck with friends from Bodrum during breakfast, lunch, and dinner.

The trip was interesting in one sense. I was in effect a Turk on a Greek island, and it gave me some insight into the problem of the Turkish minority populations in Greece and into the Turks' attitude toward the Greeks. The Greeks in Kos valued appearances and enjoyed good living. They were gay, and the Turks admired them for this, but saw them from a position of infinite moral superiority. My friends explained to me that they valued honor, and nothing more. The Greeks, said they, were dirty underneath. The Turks might wear dirty clothing, but their hearts were pure.

XIV

~~~~~

Tosun

WE LEFT for Bodrum at dusk, into the beginning of a gale, powering into the waves with the old one-cylinder engine pounding hard. When we came near land the warm wind from Anatolia struck, blowing spray that splashed off the bows hard into our faces. Then we saw the lights of Bodrum and ran the dog-leg passage near *Bardakche* in the dark.

We tied up alongside a modern steel trawler, painted battleship gray. A man in filthy khakis yelled at us in Turkish from her foredeck. "Is Peter there?"

I answered that I was indeed, and he was waiting for me as I came out of customs. Stocky and blond, he looked like Albrecht Dürer's engraving of Solyman the Magnificent. His name was Tosun Sezen, and he was well known on the coast, having made several trips with diving boats.

He introduced me to his men. Berk and Baskin were, like Tosun, graduates of Robert College, the American missionary school in Istanbul, and spoke perfect English. A fourth, Nikos, was an Istanbul Greek. When I had finished the formalities in customs, we went on board *Mercan*, the trawler, and Tosun explained his project.

Tosun thought that sponge divers should learn to use the hookah or narghile system, where the diver wears fins and a mask and uses the same type regulator that we used with our diving tanks. His air flows through a hose running from a low-pressure compressor on the surface, which is simpler and cheaper than the high-pressure machines used for filling diving tanks. Tosun had rigged a small boat as a pilot model. The greatest advantage of the narghile system was that it made decompression an economical proposition for sponge divers, since an extra regulator and hose could be used for decompression while another diver was working on the bottom. Even if the hoses got tangled, the decompressing diver could clear them easily by swimming in a circle.

Tosun had christened the little diving boat *Timurhane*, "Crazyhouse." He intended to work down the coast, using *Mercan*, the Fisheries' Commission trawler, for a depot boat, demonstrating *Timurhane*'s narghile system to sponge captains. He asked me to come along. His idea seemed good to me. I felt that the narghile system might save the sponge industry in Bodrum, and that this was one way to pay back the divers and captains of Bodrum for the wonderful things they had shown me at the bottom of the sea.

Tosun teamed up with Infidel Ali, who had once commanded deep diving boats. We experimented with *Timurhane* for a few days, and when she was running well began to work with the *manjura* system, snagging deep ledges with a grapnel and sending divers down the line. Tosun and I believed that the shocking number of fatalities in the deep diving boats before the war was the

result of sponge divers' ignorance of decompression, together with the clear impossibility of economically decompressing divers after deep dives with the heavy helmet gear. We set out to show that deep work could be
safe, if you decompressed.

With a pride of old captains and retired sponge divers
on board, *Mercan* put out one morning for a rock that
Infidel Ali knew which rose to within a hundred and
eighty feet of the surface. Tosun dived first, but the
grapnel slipped off and his dive was wasted. We dragged
again, and caught the ledge. It was my turn. With the
old men watching, I jumped over and followed the line
down.

The depth gauge strapped at my wrist said a hundred
and thirty feet, and I couldn't even see the bottom yet. I
turned and looked up at my bubbles rising, and felt reassured. The line led out and down. I continued handing
myself down it.

The ledge loomed up out of the haze, a green-gray
indistinguishable mass that came into focus as I approached. The depth gauge read one hundred and seventy feet. The rock was jagged, split by deep crevices,
covered with thin weed and "wild" sponges. I looked in
one of the crevices and saw a good commercial sponge,
gleaming black with holes in it as big around as my little
finger. There was a halo around it that made it stand out
from the others. I scratched it the way Kemal had
taught me, and the crust tore like bread under my fingernail. I got my fingers under its side and it came off easily.
I saw another. As I moved to the second, I saw a third.
There were sponges everywhere, some as big as sofa pil-
lows. I swam madly up and down the crevice like a
beggar finding money in the street.

Every sponge was proof that we could work safer and faster than divers with their big suits, heavy helmets, and necessity for by-passing decompression. I thought of them waiting in the boat above me, joking about the crazy amateurs. Only Infidel Ali believed in Tosun's idea.

I felt dizzy. The air was not coming well. I panicked for a moment, looked around, then saw that the hose was kinked. I rose ten feet and the kink came free. I turned to clear it and dashed to find more sponges. The bag was full now, and hard to carry. I swam toward a big one on top of the rock. A jerk on the hose. I swam down. Three jerks in succession. It was the signal to come up. I jerked back like a madman. "No, I won't go. There are sponges here, I'm going to get more and more."

I reached the big sponge, pulled it off, shoved it under my arm, and saw another. I jerked twice on the hose to get more slack. There was no reply. A steady pressure dragged me up and away from the rock, that beautiful rock covered wtih money. The depth gauge read a hundred and eighty feet. I looked regretfully down at the sponges disappearing under me. At a hundred feet I came to my senses and hand-over-handed up the line. I hung shivering on the shot line on my decompression stages.

It took two men to pull the bag over the gunwale of the boat. One of the Bodrum divers, Captain Ahmet, said "Bravo, Peter!" I felt like a soldier who had won a medal. They dumped my catch on the deck. There were several kilos, perhaps forty dollars' worth, all picked in ten minutes at a hundred and eighty feet. I had seen thousands of sponges before but these were mine, all mine. They were beautiful.

That evening, after Tosun and Berk had dived on the wonderful rock and picked their share, we talked excitedly with Infidel Ali and Ahmet in the cafe. Ahmet Kaptan volunteered to dive with the new equipment.

"If a crazy American and a couple of boys from Istanbul can get all those sponges, a Bodrum diver should do better!"

They talked about the times when divers deep on virgin rocks had picked twenty kilos on a dive, worth as much as a poor farmer could make in a year. Ahmet looked up. A man was coming toward us. He was bent like an old stick. He lurched painfully and slowly, one leg completely stiff and the other moving only by inches at each step. A strong cane supported him. He was about forty-five years old. Baskin turned and stopped short in the middle of a laugh.

"That's Arif," said Ahmet in a low voice, almost to the wall. Tosun stood and got a chair for him. "Ah, you should be lucky at backgammon to be a diver," Ahmet went on.

The pitiful man did not hear. He was not shy about telling his story. Twenty years before, he had been the top diver of Yahkavak village, around the peninsula from Bodrum. He had worked on *manjura* boats for six years, first as ship's boy, then as a diver, and finally as top diver. He had married one of the most beautiful girls in the district, and she had brought a good dowry. He had a good house and three children, and was adding to his wife's orange groves.

One day the grapnel caught a virgin rock at thirty-nine fathoms. Arif was the first man down. He found himself standing on a low hump of rock which rose from the bottom in a gradual curve. There were *kapa* sponges everywhere, gleaming black with ruddy gold tints. In a minute his bag was stuffed full. He unlashed his lifeline and began stringing big sponges onto it. After ten minutes they signaled him. Dopey from the great depth, he stumbled and fell while reaching for a last sponge.

"Something broke inside me," he said.

He made a normal ascent, but felt tired after they undressed him. The captain told him not to worry, that he would be all right. He was too tired to eat, and went to bed early. When he wakened the next morning, he was paralyzed from the waist down. There was no pain, and there had been no warning.

When they weighed out the sponges after drying, they found that he had gotten sixteen kilos on that last dive. They sent him home in a basket, with diapers instead of trousers. As Kemal said, with his customary delicacy about such matters, "His wife was young, but she had no children after that."

After five years Arif was better and could even walk around with a cane. He tried diving again but it did not work. He went back to his village and opened a cafe.

After Arif told his story, he asked, "Why did I get it that time? Why?"

I went to my room and got the tables. Tosun explained that even with a little cheating, the minimum decompression time at that depth would be thirty-four minutes for a ten-minute dive. You might be able to get by a few times, but against such odds you would inevitably lose.

Ahmet said, "God is big."

We went on sponge-diving, and learned what it felt like to be slightly afraid all the time. We became fascinated by sponges, those primitive animals which live by being in the right place when the sea runs by, carrying its load of micro-organisms. They grow in little colonies; where one finds one there are almost always others. A good diver knows the places where sponges should be. In deep water when we hit a colony, we always got a couple of kilos. As far as he can see, a sponge diver can tell the size of the holes and can see the glow, the slight difference in coloring which distinguishes the valuable commercial sponges from "wild" sponges.

Getting sponges became a passion with all of us and, like the Bodrum divers, we talked for hours about where they were likely to be, and how they could be gotten. Even now, when I see a sponge I pick it up, feel it, and think of the bottom from which it came.

Not all our diving this trip was done on sponge-bearing rocks. One of Infidel Ali's boats had discovered some airplanes in the sea a few years before. This had given rise to a curious attempt at a confidence game by Halil, one of the less reputable of my Bodrum friends.

Lord Kinross gives an account in *Europa Minor* of how, when he visited Bodrum in 1954, Halil tried to sell him the bodies of some British airmen. In reading Kinross's account, I see the beginning of another Bodrum big deal. Halil, as usual full of raki, must have been searching for a particularly appealing subject of conversation (Kinross was buying the raki), and was inspired by the idea of the bodies. I suppose that Kinross, being polite, acted interested enough so that Halil was certain that he was on to something big. By the time I got to Bodrum, the local version of the story was that the British government had sent Kinross, a real milord with pockets full of gold, to recover the bodies. It seems clear that these were figments of Halil's ingenious imagination. Any diver knows that even bone will disappear in the sea in a few years, unless protected in a sealed compartment where water cannot circulate, or under sediment. But Kinross had no way of knowing this. He reported Halil's offer. There was an official exchange of correspondence on the subject, and Halil drank a lot of free raki on the strength of his expectations from the "necrophile, pig-eating Englishman."

Infidel Ali offered to show us one of the planes, which lay twenty-eight fathoms deep in a cove with a sand beach at one end, a few miles from Bodrum. We had dragged the grapnel for less than a hundred feet when it hung hard on some submerged object. Tosun and I followed the line down. The water was crystal-clear. When we were still a hundred feet above the bottom we saw that the grapnel line led to a dim, dark cross which stood out clearly against the white sand. Twenty feet farther down the cross was recognizable as a two-engined bomber, tilted slightly to the right with its nose down.

It looked distressingly normal, almost like a plane parked on an airfield. Then I saw that the fabric that had covered the closely spaced metal frame of the aircraft had rotted away, and that the whole structure was covered with sponges. A big *kapa* sponge grew on each of the three radio aerials which ran down the middle of the fuselage. I picked them and shoved them into the bag, and swam the length of the fuselage, over the nose of the plane, until I stood on the sand, gazing up at the nose and the engine nacelles. The left propeller was feathered and undamaged. The right engine had been running when they hit the water, and its propeller was bent.

Woozy from the depth, I tried hard to concentrate, to remember that I wanted to find a serial number to identify the plane. Deciding to look in the cockpit for an instrument, I discovered the reason the outline of the plane seemed strange. The cockpit was broken off clean. I looked into the place where the cockpit had been and saw only a buckled seat beside a mass of radio gear. This was solidly attached, so I swam to the sand between the engines, where some bits of wreckage protruded, hoping to find the instrument panel. The first thing that came to my hand was a round object, buried in the sand. I pulled. It was the pilot's control wheel. It was attached to the wreck by blackened rusty wires, which broke easily. I dug in the sand and found the foot pedals.

I felt the signal and swam up regretfully with the wheel in my hand. On the decompression stop I took out my knife to clean the wheel, and with horror realized what must have happened to the pilot. What I had thought was sea growth was the charred leather that had covered the wheel. Fire had stained the vanadium steel tubing of the wheel itself.

The pilot had played a poor hand well, but lost his gamble. He must have been hit over German-occupied Kos or Rhodes. On fire with one engine out, losing altitude, he headed for the Turkish coast and Keramos Bay, where he knew that there was a good chance of being picked up by the British MTB's which used it for an operations base. The cove with the sandy beach was an ideal place for ditching. He was probably too low to parachute, and parachuting into the sea was risky anyhow. Better ditch. Losing altitude, cockpit burning, he made his approach.

Then something happened. Perhaps he was blinded by

fire, maybe the controls were burnt away. Perhaps he just died. In the last minute she went out of control and banged into the water. The nose broke off and she sank, taking the crew with her. The men in the smashed cock-pit must have died instantly. Those aft might have lived a little longer, but not much. The hatches were still sealed tight until Tosun pried them off next day.

We never learned the name of that brave pilot, because we couldn't find an identifying piece with a legible serial number. We were sorry. Somewhere in England, someone would like to know.

We pulled into the harbor at evening promenade time. In front of the police station a crowd was circling a battered passenger car, its roof piled unreasonably high with dusty bulging bundles. A large pair of feet protruded from the rear window. They disappeared and were replaced by a face just visible behind a large beard. The door of the car burst open and I saw why the crowd was staring so. The man who jumped out was wearing what was surely the loudest sport shirt ever seen in Bodrum.

Tosun whistled. "Who is it?"

"That's Gigi."

Jean Jacques Flori had arrived. His sport shirt, part of the collection acquired on a trip around Africa as cameraman on *Calypso*, was as successful in Bodrum as it had been in Afghanistan and Assam. His companion, Claude Duthuit, had just been released from the French army in Algeria, and was also a diver.

We went to the *gasinosu*, ate and drank too much, and exchanged news. They had just finished a documentary film after having been held up for six weeks by customs in Istanbul, where all their possessions had been impounded, including clothes and car. They volunteered on the spot for sponge-diving in *Timurhane*.

In the middle of dinner the postman came by with a bundle of letters for me. I was putting them unread into my pocket when I noticed "Government of Cyprus" on one of the envelopes. I opened it. It was from Andrew Megaw, director of the Cyprus Department of Antiquities, and it said in part:

From the descriptions you give, I have no doubt that this is an important find of Cypriot copper ingots of the late Bronze Age. Sir Bernard Burroughs* is to be congratulated on spotting the similarity of the ingots to that exhibited in the Cyprus Museum.

This was official confirmation. I had assumed, from a hasty reference to library books, that we had found a Bronze Age ship, but that was only an amateur guess. Now it was certain that the bronze wreck was really what I had believed it was since the day that Kemal, sitting at that very table, had told the story of the ingots in the sea and the phrase "rotten bronze" had stuck in my mind. The archaeologists would have to listen now, because what lay at Cape Gelidonya could not be ignored.

It got to be a good party. Everyone liked Claude and Gigi. A large white mongrel dog sensed the general feeling of brotherliness and attached himself to Gigi, who reciprocated with bread soaked in raki. At dawn we all, dog included, swayed and stumbled home.

It would be misguided to describe how we felt when

---

* Who had visited Bodrum and the museum, and suggested that I write Megaw.

I pried Claude and Gigi out of bed and dragged them down the street, praising with hypocritical enthusiasm the standard Bodrum breakfast of meatballs, hot peppers, and tomatoes.

We turned a corner and Gigi gasped. The street was littered with dead dogs, victims of the annual anti-rabies campaign. In the gutter was stretched Gigi's friend "Whitey," very still. Near him another mongrel lay dying, contorted in the last stages of strychnine poisoning.

"Poor Whitey." Gigi was almost in tears.

We went sadly down the street, whatever small appetite we might have had for breakfast completely spoiled. "Dead dog" Whitey got up and trotted after us, saved by a colossal hangover. He too must have had little appetite that morning when the policeman offered him the poisoned meat.

Claude and Gigi learned fast. Soon they knew where to look in the crevices of rocks for a sponge, and how to spot the little raised mound and the central tendril of yellow grass that marked where a sponge might be hidden under high eelgrass.

We worked close to Bodrum, so that we could demonstrate *Timurhane's* technique to a new set of captains, divers, or boat owners every day. It was pleasant to sleep in a bed, and I wallowed in village luxuries: hot tea and sweet cakes, which replaced calories lost in the cold water and which we all craved.

We were always cold. We often had aching hands, especially when we had been deep and used one hand for pulling a difficult sponge off a rock. I had lost a great deal of weight after four months of hard diving, and was tired all the time. Usually I sat still, indifferent to everything, but sometimes I found myself unreasonably irritable and difficult.

I was sustained by the divers' growing respect for the equipment which they had at first dismissed as a toy; by the warm, hopeful knowledge that the Gelidonya wreck was waiting for us to excavate it; and by the amount of information about other ancient shipwrecks which poured in from the divers who came in the evenings to discuss the new style of diving. Now, in November, most of the Bodrum boats were back from the coast. Only Captain Kemal stayed at sea, fanatic as ever in his search for sponges.

Tosun pleaded with the customs for permission to use the decompression chamber. The answer was, as always, *yok*. It was horrible to dive with the feeling that if something happened and one of us were to get the bends, he might die because of one official's greed.

Tosun and I spent days trying to telephone Ankara in order to get a minister or deputy to ask the Customs Ministry to allow the Fisheries Ministry to use the chamber, against a guarantee that it would be re-exported. It was hopeless. If we had had two or three months, it might have been possible, but not now with winter coming on. We continued deep diving, wary of the Damoclean sword hanging over us.

The sun lost its warmth from day to day, and there were shivers of icy wind from the north. The children of the town ran and shouted in their blue school uniforms. Even Hussein, the cafe owner, abandoned his reluctant shamble of summer.

Perhaps because I was tired, perhaps because I had lost my emotional balance after the surrealistic frustrations of the summer, I did a very foolish thing. The official leader of Tosun's expedition was a representative of the Fisheries Commission, whom I will call Ahmet. He was a political appointee whose only interest in his job was apparently what he could steal from the small fishing boats, imported from Europe at the expense of the Food and Agricultural Organization of the United Nations. They said that he had pimped for the American soldiers in Istanbul before his father had managed to finagle him into the Fisheries Commission.

He could not stop Tosun because Tosun had enough political influence with which to threaten him. He could, however, make life remarkably difficult. He moved a mattress to the cabin top of *Mercan* and slept there during the day while we were diving, waking occasionally to make unpleasant remarks.

One day Gigi and Claude dived, wearing tanks, over *Mercan's* side. When they were in the water he remarked loudly, "Hidedoo, there go the crazy pig-eaters."

I was on deck, suited up with tanks on my back. "Repeat that," I said.

He said nothing. I slipped the tanks off and asked him again. He told me to go to hell, and said that if I weren't wearing my diver's knife, he would come down and teach me a lesson in manners.

I threw the knife to him and leapt after it. He fumbled. I was on him before he had it well in his hand. My thumbs were about to meet on his windpipe when they pried us apart. Tosun kicked him off the boat, and we headed for the Chattals for a last bout of sponge-diving.

It was almost December. Silt from the first rains had clouded the water weeks before, and the sea was gray.

Kayf came naturally to all of us. Our bodies were still able to obey commands, but neither willingly nor easily. When we sat, we didn't move, even to light cigarettes. It was an effort to talk, to go on with anything. A day free from diving was like lifting a rucksack from one's shoulders after walking hard miles with it.

We were working the grass for sponges. The north wind blew. Finally we ran to shelter under big Karabaglar. Kemal was already anchored there, like us unable to stand the cold.

I rowed over in the dinghy to find all *Mandalinche*'s crew tucked cheerfully in the covered hold with the compressor, like mice in a nest. They made room for me. Kiasim, as usual, lit me a smoke and began cracking almonds with the rusty pliers. Kemal, asleep in the *rancha*, shouted his welcome, and I heard him bumbling around inside.

An old diver, Uncle Sali, chuckled, got up, and worked his way past the compressor till he reached the overhead where something wrapped in a white cloth, long and slim like a rifle, hung suspended. Kiasim turned to me, smiling his wintry old diver's smile.

"Sali will play for us, and the hell with the wind."

Kemal crawled bearlike out of the *rancha* with a bottle of raki in his hand, and we went up onto the foredeck, where Sali unwrapped the cloth and took out a slim, lutelike instrument. He hunched against the cabin and played old, old tunes. Kemal sat in his usual place, leaning against the breasthooks of the bows like a pirate king. Then, with the wind howling around the collar of his dirty old coat, Kemal told the story of his teacher, Ali Kaptan, from Bozburnu, who had taken him as ship's boy nearly thirty years ago in the bad old days

[165]

of the *fernez*. Ali Kaptan had died at thirty fathoms. The compressor had quit, his suit was ripped at the breastplate, and he drowned before they could get him to the surface. They buried him on Yassi Ada.

I began to understand why Kemal hated the place. Ali's little boat, an *aktarma* like *Mandalinche*, had anchored in the bay out of the *meltem*. The frightened men, stumbling under the burden of their dead captain, had struggled to the top of the island and, in the sweeping wind, had tried to hack a grave deep enough to keep the body from the hungry rats. I remembered them running over my blanket, and shivered.

We all had sores which were always open because of continual immersion in salt water. I had several, on both hands and feet. One day I awoke with a high fever, the sores inflamed and running pus, with streaks of red leading from them toward my heart. I collapsed in bed and stayed there, sustained by massive injections of antibiotics by my friend, the doctor.

Ahmet the Pimp didn't waste a moment of the opportunity offered by his enemy's weakness. He got alongside the harbormaster, and that official suddenly noticed that *Mercan* was not licensed to carry passengers. As we were foreigners and could not be issued Turkish seamen's certificates, Tosun was forbidden to take us out with him.

Nikos, the Greek boy from Istanbul, was "grounded" for the same reason. In his case it would have been lucky if the harbormaster's decision to forbid him to dive had not been overruled by Tosun's political friends. He returned with Tosun the next year and the year after, and during the third summer he died in the decompression chamber that Tosun finally managed to install in Bodrum.

His death was pitiful and was a shocking illustration of the barbarity and inhumanity of which the Turks are accused by their Greek neighbors. As Nikos lay dying, someone told me later, an educated Turk from Istanbul was heard to say that he hoped Nikos would die, because he was a dirty Greek. It was also rumored that he had been murdered, by being kept too deep too long.

Left without divers, Tosun's experiment stopped. Tosun laughed ruefully when I told him the story of what had happened to Newton, the English archaeologist who had excavated the Mausoleum a hundred years before. Some lions which had decorated the Mausoleum had been built into the castle walls. Newton got the British government to apply for a permit from the Sultan to remove them, in order to prevent their being further damaged. The permit was delayed, but, before long, Newton was shocked to see the commandant of the castle removing the lions. He sent frantic messages to the British Minister in Constantinople. Meanwhile, the commandant would appear at the excavation site to remark politely, "You have found nothing but little fragments, I see!"

Newton lost his temper. He cursed the commandant in English, much as I had cursed the customs officials that day in Istanbul, and raged through the streets of Bodrum, as I had done during the great decompression-chamber negotiations.

The commandant got six lions out of the walls, wrapped them in sheepskins, and loaded them onto the caïque which was to take them to Kos to be transferred to the Constantinople steamer. We laughed, imagining

Newton fuming, as he watched the poorly wrapped parcels being lumped onto the dock by soldiers, fearful that the careless Turks would smash them.

The night before the caïque sailed, the firman arrived. At six in the morning, the English archaeologist called on the commandant, who was not yet dressed. Newton says, "I put the firman into his hand with the air of satisfaction with which a whist player trumps an ace . . ."

The commandant smiled, that goddamn condescending smile, and remarked that the permit specified lions, but the statues were really leopards. However, Newton had an English man-of-war in the harbor behind him. The commandant backed down. The lions are now in the British Museum. Fortunately for both the customs director and the harbormaster, we had no warship anchored in the harbor.

Ahmet the Pimp was now boasting to waterfront hangers-on that he would "fix" Tosun. Like Newton, we were in a race against time, for soon bad weather would make it impossible to dive. By this time Tosun also needed a replacement crew for *Mercan*. The captain, cook, and engineer, all sailors from the Bosporus, were in a state of near mutiny induced by Ahmet. Captain Kemal and Infidel Ali suggested that we send them back to Istanbul in disgrace and replace them with Bodrum men, but Tosun rightly said that it was better to have them under control in Bodrum than loose in Istanbul, telling lies to the Fisheries Commission.

I lay in state, with my sores. On the first day thirty visitors came to see me. Uncle Kiasim and Kemal came, hats in hand, looking so doleful that I laughed. Kiasim sat on the bed, lighting cigarettes and handing them to me, smiling his secret old man's smile and winking confidentially. They came back later in the day, spectacularly drunk and hardly able to stand. Kemal stood swaying at the foot of the bed and cried.

"Karagoez Amja [black-eyed uncle], all the good divers are dead, and look at you!" He patted my swollen hands.

Claude Duthuit walked in and remarked, "Kee-rist, it's lucky we're not in Greece. They'd be worshipping you with those stigmata."

The sores were in about the right place. Claude and I roared, then spent the next hour trying to explain to Kemal what stigmata were.

I had never worn shoes in Bodrum, only the same old pair of battered sandals. The doctor remarked to a storekeeper that perhaps my feet had become infected because of this. The merchant, a former sponge-boat owner, came to tell me that he had lots of shoes in his store, and if I wanted a free pair I should come around, when I could walk.

The doctor was married, a good Moslem, in general a moral man. He shocked me once by asking me if I wanted to meet a nice boy, rather in the manner that a friend in the States or Europe would say, "I know a nice girl you should meet."

Once the subject of atrocities came up. I mentioned a case I had heard about. In the Dardanelles a trench which had been overrun by the Turks had then been recaptured by the British, and some of the British dead had been found raped. The doctor was shocked.

"Turks would never do a thing like that," he said. "They must have raped them first, then shot them."

He was outraged when I told him what a late eighteenth-century Frenchman had put into the mouth of the ancient Greek writer Anacharsis, when he published what purported to be a translation from previously unknown writings. It was, of course, a fake, inspired by the dying eighteenth century's desire to believe in "la nouvelle Cythère." Halicarnassus was presented as that earthly paradise, where there were only

the most enticing women, and the celebrations at the Salmacis fountain inspire only indolence, abandon, and voluptuousness . . . This peninsula is, perhaps, the most enticing, the most voluptuous, of all the regions of the Aegean sea . . . The young *Halicarnassiennes*, retained by the government in order to profess in public the art of sensual joy . . . recline on flowery lawns, offering their open arms to all who visit this terrestrial paradise . . .

The doctor protested, "Such a thing could never happen in Bodrum! We wouldn't allow it." He went on to say that this was what one would expect of Greeks. He then described one of his most interesting cases, the autopsy of an old man which demonstrated that he had been murdered, anally, with a screwdriver.

"You see, we are law-abiding people here," he explained. "Our only crimes are those of passion."

It was very cold, and there was no hope of getting the harbormaster to reconsider his order forbidding us to dive that year. Tosun sailed for Istanbul, and Jean Jacques and Claude, after a week of waiting for Mustafa to come from Izmir, left also. Kemal's wife began cooking for

TOSUN

me. In the afternoons, Kemal would bring his oldest
daughter, Shukran, aged about five, to cuddle in his arms
while he and I talked. It was strange to see him, the
grim captain, with a child in his arms. Her name meant
"Thank you."

When I could walk, he used to take me to his house,
where I sat in the courtyard and was served by his patient wife with all manner of delicacies involving yogurt. My pleasure was almost as great as his own at
watching Shukran stagger across the courtyard, very
serious, with a big plate of food.

I had no money at all. I borrowed from Kemal, and
waited. Finally a telegram came from America saying
that money had been sent, and that the *National Geographic* wanted me to write an article about the Bronze
Age ship.

This was success of a kind. I knew that what Mustafa
and I had begun would continue, but that everything
would be different. I had had a rare experience in living
and working with Kemal and his men, and in living in
the town, but this could not be repeated. I would be
back with an expedition, and when I returned my relationship with the Bodrum men would change.

I arranged for a passage to Kos, from where I would
go to Kalymnos to be alone and write the article, against
the deadline in the telegram. The day the boat left I
packed my gear, then tottered up the mountain to the
rock-cut tomb where I had sat so many times. Looking
down at the town, the castle, and the sea beyond, I
thought of the many Bodrums I had known.

The Bodrum of the modern Greeks still lives, though
they left forty years ago. There are oil drums stored in
their churches now, instead of women kneeling in black

dresses. There is the Bodrum of the old Turks, praying in the mosque, and the new Bodrum, modern Turkey if you like, with its officials and flags and attempts to be modern: the ice plant, the new dock, the Sunday promenade in pointed shoes, *Hayat* magazine on the barbershop chair, the newfangled girls' school, and loudspeakers blaring.

The fisherman, smuggler, and sponge diver know one Bodrum and the farmers another, but they touch at many points. The divers farm the sea to get money, to buy land so that their sons can go to school and wear shiny pointed shoes in the Bodrum of the future.

Sensed in the background but seldom seen is the Bodrum of the women, glimpsed peeping through their closed shutters, or gardening, or hurrying through the dirty streets from one clean room where women chatter and sew to another like it.

Looming over everything is the past: the Crusaders' castle, bits of antique frieze in a wall, a Corinthian column used for a bollard or holding up the arbor of a café. The pattern of the houses is not very different from what it must always have been; and the lines of the ancient harbor are just visible under the dirty water of the modern port.

Then there are the ghosts who people Bodrum in the late watches of the night and during the hot, still summer afternoons, forgotten by the Turks, but still able to move us: Mausolus, whose image now stares insolently down a gallery of the British Museum far away in London; Alexander the Great, who must have read the writings of Herodotus of Halicarnassus and who sacked the town; Cicero, who rehabilitated the town after it had fallen to decay; Vitruvius, the careful Roman architect, who would surely enjoy the company of Osman Bey, director of education and the Turgut school, who is also careful and exact and a gentle man; and Scylax of Caryanda, who under a Persian king opened the sea routes to the east and who might have drunk Koan wine near the beach where Kemal and I had planned another kind of voyage.

An old caïque, confiscated somewhere on the coast from a Samian Greek and now run by Turks who obviously didn't care, moldered in the bay where once lay the black ships of Minos and the swift penteconters of Anthes, the warlord from Troezen who first fortified the castle rock and hellenized the district. The Barbary corsairs, British battleships, and stout round ships of the Levant Company are forgotten, but some names still ring and rumble, and touch chords very close us: John Kendall, and Henry Schlegleholt, who wondered at sculptures from the Mausoleum before he burnt them into lime to rebuild the castle and who, if he thought about it at all, would likely justify himself with the complacent Germanic platitude that "a soldier has to perform his duty." Some of the Englishmen who kept watch on that fortress had grandsons and nephews who settled in Virginia: Nevill, Percy, Strange, Talbot, Stafford, De Vere, Courtenay, Fitzhugh, Hallestowe.

On the way down the mountain I saw a broken amphora in a trash heap at the edge of town, a little past the orchard where the Mausoleum had stood. It was one of the types Miss Grace had taught me to identify, a Rhodian of the third century before Christ. Picked up by a diver or a trawler, it had resumed for a time its function as the common vessel for which the potter had shaped it over two thousand years ago. Now it had come to an unsentimental end among the rest of the village rubbish.

I hobbled back down to the town. It was time to go. After interminable formalities, we cast off. The old boat drifted for a minute under the grim battlements of the Crusaders' castle, until they got her in gear. Then we headed for Kos at five knots, rotten bulwarks palpitating with vibration, in a cloud of diesel fumes. The black-shawled Turkish women in the cabin began retching before we had passed the breakwater, and the ship's boy flung a bucket down the hatch, which was greeted by a wail, either thanks or a curse. On the opposite course came a diving boat, an unshaven character in a rumpled lounge suit at the tiller. Her diving ladder, folded to the starboard shrouds, was an actual as well as a symbolic link between us and the tantalizing depths of the sea which we were entering.

The water turned clear blue, and I leaned on the quivering forestay and dreamed of all the ships lost in that romantic sea, of Mycenean galleys, triremes, *naves onerariae*, dromons, cutters, ketches, *saykes*, *vomvarthas*, brigs, barks, *trechendiris*, the fast *kerkuroi* of Rhodes of Alexander's time, whose name lives in the humble fishing boats of the islands; line-of-battle ships; crumbling destroyers from World War II, their guns still trained upward toward the aircraft which sank them; submarines, their sleek hulls and beautiful complicated machinery dissolving into original elements; great cargo ships, hatches blown upward and davits out, with giant groupers inhabiting holds where stevedores sweated. All of them lost, some in gales, others smashed on reefs through bad luck, foolishness, too much advice, lack of judgment, excess of caution, barratry, or bad construction. Others had been torpedoed, bombed, rammed, burnt, and sailed under. They were all there, waiting, some for me, some for the ones who would come after, and two hundred miles to the south, at Gelidonya, the Cape of Swallows, the bronze wreck waited too.

XV

∽∽∽∽∽

Mounting the Expedition

I ARRIVED in New York in the middle of a snowstorm the day before Christmas. For two years I had corresponded with John Huston, founder and secretary of the Council of Underwater Archaeology. He had written to Dr. Rodney Young of the University of Pennsylvania Museum, whose interest had first been aroused by verification of the age of several bronze tools from the Gelidonya wreck. These had been taken as souvenirs by the Cochrans, without my knowledge or Hakki Bey's, and examined by Professor Eric Sjoquist of Princeton.*

After Christmas, at the Archaeological Congress in New York, I told my story to Dr. Young and to Dr. Machteld Mellink of Bryn Mawr, pleading urgency with as much vehemence as possible. The Bodrum divers would never allow a known salvage job, with its two tons of scrap metal, to lie unmolested. Delay meant that the wreck would be destroyed, like three other Bronze Age shipwrecks dynamited by the sponge divers in the

---

* The souvenirs caused a lot of trouble for me later. They were seen on an American TV program by a Turkish official, and I was accused in the Turkish press of smuggling antiquities. The objects have since been returned to Bodrum, and the charges dropped.

last fifty years. They listened patiently to my anxious babble about "dozens of ancient wrecks," then introduced me to a young man who had been sitting quietly at one corner of the table.

"Work all this into some kind of program and come to see us next week," said Dr. Young, and left me with George Bass, who was then a research assistant at the University Museum.

George's first question was characteristic. "Do you think I'll have trouble learning to dive?"

"Not unless there's something wrong with you," I answered.

He grinned. "There better not be."

He had a decent face, very open, a high-pitched Southern drawl, and curiously innocent mannerisms. He was the kind of man to whom a bank manager would lend money. We went up to my loft on 31st Street with a bottle of bourbon, and talked until dawn. We found that we had both been in the Far East in the army, George as a lieutenant running a radio detachment on the 38th parallel, and I as a sergeant running small ships. We had both been fascinated with archaeology since childhood, but George had taken the straight path, with seven years of study behind him. He felt that the Cape Gelidonya wreck might be material for a doctoral dissertation. He had worked on excavations for several seasons and was full of ideas. He had no patience with compromise in his approach to the methodical reconstruction of history.

Compared with George I was an amateur. I knew much more than he did about the practical aspects of the expedition because my experience had been practical. I still had a strong desire to be an archaeologist, with or without the academic right to do so. The one thing that we were never to disagree about, the thing which made our relationship an unusual one, was that our feelings about archaeology were the same.

George was engaged to a beautiful Southern girl named Ann. She came and brewed coffee for us while we thrashed out our working program, which Dr. Young approved at the end of the week. The University Museum granted us an immediate $10,000. This sum was about half what we needed for a minimum budget. With four months to go until we would have to leave for Turkey, we set to work to raise funds and borrow equipment.

Some of the people we talked to were supercilious, and others were insulting. Underwater archaeology was something for the men's magazines. One magazine editor pointed to a photograph of a beautiful girl, whose charms were very little altered by air tanks strapped on her back. Another regretted not supporting us, but told us to be sure to come back if we ever found a treasure ship. I suggested that a ship of the time of the Trojan wars was more interesting than treasure. But it was difficult to explain that we meant to use diving only as a tool of archaeology. We meant to work underwater, not just salvage things for archaeologists to study on land. Few people understood. We were a bunch of skin divers off on a summer adventure and nothing more.

We were in fact attempting something that had not been done before, an archaeological excavation conducted underwater according to land standards. Our most revolutionary idea was to draw a plan underwater, for much of the meaning of the cargo of the wreck at Gelidonya would be learned through studying the context in which objects were found.

Unlike most earlier attempts at underwater excavation, we were not supported by a navy or by a government, but by a small group of people who eventually formed a kind of committee. Harry Starr, director of the Littauer Foundation, promised us cash if his board approved, and his intelligent questions clarified ideas which helped us raise other funds. Walter Feinberg of the Boston Sea Rovers, one of the pioneer East Coast divers, introduced us to manufacturers and thus made large discounts on equipment possible for us. Nixon Griffis, now president of the American branch of the World Council of Underwater Activities, and James Dugan, Captain Jacques-Yves Cousteau's literary associate, formed an advisory board which kept us out of trouble in the early days of organizing the expedition.

The equipment list was staggering. We had to build a camp for twenty people. The island nearest the wreck was so steep that we would have had to dynamite the rock to make a level place, and to raise concrete platforms for men and machinery. We decided to build our camp on a mainland beach.

We planned to process all our photographs the day they were taken so that drawings made underwater could be checked against them. This meant including all the equipment and supplies for a darkroom, and involved problems not immediately apparent. Could film be washed in salt water? Our fresh water supply would be limited. The Kodak people said salt water was all right, if the final bath was fresh. Another technical question was that of developing photographic film at a temperature of 98 degrees instead of 68. This we solved by adding a special chemical to the developer. If we were to print photographs, we had to have an enlarger. What enlarger was tough enough to do heavy duty in primitive conditions, yet small enough to be fairly portable? It would require a generator or batteries to run the light, and the darkroom itself needed darkroom lights. Peter Laye, salesman for Medo Photo Supply, spent days hunting down the right enlarger and then persuaded his company to let us have it and all the rest of our photographic equipment on credit.

I was technical adviser to George, and yet I had never worked with an air lift, one of the essential tools in underwater archaeology. I telephoned all over the East Coast trying to find someone who had used one, and finally got information from the naval diving establishment in Washington.

The budget stood up poorly to our demands upon it. We had $3000 with which to buy $30,000 worth of equipment. We redoubled our assaults on manufacturers. U.S. Divers gave us a large discount on diving equipment. The Nikon Company loaned us a newly developed underwater case and cameras to go with it. The Polaroid Corporation lent us a camera. At Dumas' urging, OFRS, Captain Cousteau's research laboratory in Marseilles, built an underwater case for it. A diver could photograph an object on the bottom, surface, and show the print to George Bass, so that he could make an immediate decision on how to handle it.

Honor Frost recruited Miss Joan du Plat Taylor. Miss Taylor had been an assistant curator of the Cyprus Museum. She found funds for a draftsman and photographer, together with their transportation and her own. Herb Greer, an old friend and expedition companion, wired that he could come along as photographer.

By March the expedition was in shape: George Bass,

director; Miss Taylor, assistant to George in charge of preservation of objects and pottery; myself, technical adviser and acting assistant director; Frederic Dumas, chief diver; Honor Frost, architect; Captain Kemal Aras, running the boats; Herb Greer, photographer; and Claude Duthuit, diver and assistant to Dumas. Every person on the original crew was along because of a specific skill. The only members of the crew who had not worked on a land excavation were Greer, Dumas, Duthuit, and Captain Kemal, and both Dumas and Duthuit had worked on underwater excavations. Peter Dorrell, photographer, and Terry Ball, draftsman, who were to join us in July, both had a lot of experience on land digs.

George married Ann a few weeks before we sailed for Europe. She was to meet us in Turkey in a month or two, when she had finished college. The day before George left Philadelphia, one of his colleagues remarked that he envied George the nice honeymoon he was going to have, lazing on the beach, swimming and sunbathing.

XVI

~~~~~

The Beyannami

WE ARRIVED in Istanbul in April, 1960, to find the manifests for all our equipment waiting for us, but no permit. We headed for Ankara to see what had happened. A suave gentleman in the Department of Antiquities informed us that the permit had been started through "channels." We inquired what those channels might be.

"First it has to be signed by all the subministries, then by each cabinet minister, and finally by the prime minister and the president. It shouldn't take more than three months."

George gasped. "Three months from *now?*"

"Oh no, from last week."

We visited one of the top men in the American embassy. He hated, he said, to be the first to tell us, but it seemed unlikely that our permit would come through that year. He had spoken about our case to a high official in the Department of Antiquities.

That worthy had told him that "Turkey is not ready for underwater archaeology, which is, in any case, not very important or interesting. We archaeologists are interested in the culture of the people, not in minor details like ship construction, which is of interest only to a few specialists."

The reply, that a ship was as much evidence of a people's culture as a house, stuck in our throats. It would never get back to the official, who would not have listened anyway.

We scrabbled sycophantically in Ankara's dingy corridors of power. It took a week to reach the presence of the Minister of Customs, after the Department of Antiquities agreed to tell the customs that we had the Department's permission for an expedition.

That day the streets were full of students carrying placards. We passed truckloads of riot police. The government closed all colleges and universities "till fall." It was hard to find out what was happening, since the local press contained only government propaganda, the foreign papers were always three or four days late, and any mention of Turkey had been excised.

We went to Istanbul to begin extracting our tons of equipment from customs, not at all encouraged by a man whom we met the day before we left. An astronomer on his way home from a two-year contract to teach at Ankara University and to set up an observatory there, he had not yet been able to extract from customs the telescope that had been sent out to him from California. There was, it appeared, no customs regulation covering the import of telescopes.

The broker recommended to us welcomed us with unpleasant effusion. We drank tea while he dwelt at length on his intimate acquaintance with the highest officers in the customs, and his skill at the art of the *Beyannami*. He went on at length until George asked what a *Beyannami* was.

"The document, my dears, that you must fill out before your equipment can enter Turkey."

He extracted a paper folder from a desk drawer. It was the size and shape of a tabloid newspaper. We gasped. The first page required eighty-three entries. There were sixteen pages.

He sent us, accompanied by an assistant, to open the cases in the presence of an "inspector." The first step, he said, was to write in Turkish a description of each item, since most of our equipment had never been seen in Turkey.

Item: butterfly valve (part of an aqualung).

With the optimism of the amateur, I looked up "butterfly" in the Turkish dictionary. The man brightened, then gestured in bewilderment at the tiny rubber valves. I demonstrated the action of a butterfly valve with my lips.

"Poo pap, poo pap!" I panted anxiously.

"Poo pap, poo pap!" He joined me. Our breathy chorus continued until he resumed his air of inquisitor. "Of course," he remarked, "butterflies don't go poo pap."

We spent an hour explaining that once upon a time someone elsewhere must have thought the action of the valve resembled that of the wings of a butterfly. At last he noted down the official description: "Valve that goes poo pap to keep the water out."

We went through four days and hundreds of items, each described surrealistically in illegible longhand by the inspector, and then spent two more days feeding seals, stamps, and irrelevant information into the voracious *Beyannami*. At the end of the week we found that our Poo Pap tormentor was not, as we had thought, a customs inspector, but only an employee of the broker. We had not yet approached the threshold of customs.

Like the man who first begins to suspect his wife, we at first ignored, then avoided the evidence of perfidy which was obvious to everyone. Our broker was making our customs clearance as long and complex as possible in order to earn the huge fee he meant to charge us.

Tosun took us to meet the politician who had made the *Timurhane* expedition possible. "There are no normal channels in Turkey," he said. "Tell your broker to call me."

The broker insisted in his turn that we must go through the "correct" channels. "We experts must take care of it. Things must run their normal course."

We slaved for two more days until the *Beyannami* was completed to his satisfaction. It was a handsome document. It included:

16 signatures, notarized and witnessed by George Bass
10 tax stamps
28 ink block stamps
35 initials, from six or seven different people
8 official signatures, witnessed
4 red wax seals with the official customs seal on them (the
    seals were to attach copies of four official letters,
    each one of which had one initial, one stamp, and
    another signature by George Bass)
9 pages of additional documents, containing:
    17 ink block stamps
    3 paper stamps
    11 signatures of verification.

Pinned to the official form, the pins stuck solid with sealing wax, was a heavy bundle of paper, handwritten and almost completely illegible. A dozen of these pages contained descriptions laboriously made by Poo Pap. Six or seven pages more contained abstruse mathematical calculations which did not relate to anything either George or I understood.

Attached in another place was a bundle of letters, also pinned and sealed. There were letters from the embassy, letters from the Department of Antiquities, letters from faceless people in departments with unreasonable names, from directors in chief, directors, sub-directors, and assistants to sub-directors.

The thing was ornamented with colored tax stamps of various denominations with pictures of factories on them, either factories that the government meant to build or ones already constructed in outlying districts. These last were part of the pork-barrel policy of the party in power, and many of them now stood idle for lack of materials which could not be imported because of customs regulations. Those stamps had lost us at least three days, for we were always having to run half a mile just before closing to buy a special one to authorize someone's signature.

"They were right about the Boston tea party," George remarked, and I was struck by what my Turkish friends would have described as a dangerous thought, that revolutions may have less to do with patriotism than with sheer frustration.

That night the army imposed a six o'clock curfew on Istanbul. Tosun, trapped in our hotel, told horrible stories of students who were being tortured, some to death, by the police.

We had an appointment with the Sub-Director of Customs at nine o'clock in the morning. We found his office occupied only by a monstrous bust of Ataturk, the great reformer, the presence which dominated every official precinct in Turkey. I looked gloomily at it.

"He reformed the government and the army and brought Turkey into the modern world, but why didn't he reform the customs?"

I knew the sad answer. "His father was a customs official."

Just then the Sub-Director of Customs arrived escorted by a covey of sycophants. Our broker, using his two hundred and fifty pounds as a battering ram, was first to the desk. We swept into the presence in his wake. He bowed and deposited the paper on the desk. George and I stood at parade rest, trying to look harmless, innocent, deserving.

The great man read a paragraph or two. Without raising his head he said, "Yok."

"But why?" George was exploding. "He has to tell us *why!*"

The broker turned to go. I repeated it in Turkish. The great man favored the broker with a three-minute tongue-lashing and flung our beautiful *Beyannami* aside onto an unsteady tower of similar documents on his desk.

The broker led us out of the office. "Of course you must realize that this is a difficult case, but for a slight extra fee, I'll handle it myself."

"But what about the *Beyannami?*" we asked.

"Oh," said he, "it was not correct. We must begin again."

George flushed and his eye caught Ataturk's, staring from a huge portrait which hung in the main office over a heap of bundled papers that reached nearly to the ceiling. We escaped from the broker, pleading a previous appointment, and collapsed outside into hysterical laughter that made the miserable street ring and turned a hundred sour faces in our direction.

We joked all through the teeming streets of Beyoglu. I remarked that Turkey was not really a country at all, but something the Deity had invented to punish people with. And, indeed, in the late Middle Ages this doctrine had actually been preached. We leaned against the wall of a sixteenth-century Genoese warehouse and roared. Two cops came toward us, tommy guns loose on their shoulders. Laughter was rare in that district. We looked at the expressionless Central Asian faces and walked faster up the hill.

We were in real trouble. In normal times, we might have found a way to do things, but with a revolution and perhaps civil war around the corner, what hope was there?

Our friend in court was at home, and called the director, who agreed to receive us at nine the next morning. We woke late and took a taxi to the customs house, racing to be on time.

The director arrived just before noon, sniffing a rose. We were ushered in almost immediately and introduced to a gentleman who busied himself with tea and occasional sniffs of the director's rose. A lot of talk revealed that he was an ex-customs official who might write us another *Beyannami*. All he wanted was five hundred dollars — cash. In advance.

Luckily, it was time for lunch. We ran to the telephone and found Tosun, who called our protector, who called the customs director, who promised under duress that he would allow us to clear customs, protesting that it was all illegal.

The under-inspector of customs assigned to our case was a liver-lipped creature who crouched behind his dirty desk like a horned toad waiting for flies. I said a silent prayer of thanks that this man had been sent as a helper, not as an enemy. He was nice to us, in his gruesome way. He did not feel the need to order us a cup of tea, a good sign meaning he was not going to tell us *yok*.

He summoned a starved-looking little man in a brown coat with soup stains down its front, who wore very old-fashioned round-rimmed eyeglasses. We set out at an aggressive trot with a new blank *Beyannami* and a note scribbled by Liverlips in red ink.

We sped through anterooms where we had cooled our heels so long. Once one of our opponents called Liverlips, to question the incredible news that things were officially being made easy for us. We heard confused shouting, distorted over the telephone. Our chastened opponent hung up, signed, and stamped the paper.

"Highly irregular," he remarked. "All these papers are waiting." He gestured to a dusty heap of forms on the concrete floor beside his desk.

That afternoon there were more demonstrations. We sat in the gloomy hotel lobby watching tanks knock corners off shops. On Monday Soupstain was ill. On Tuesday the government ordered a national holiday for all government workers. On Wednesday neither Liverlips nor Soupstain was there.

We felt like frightened children in the dark, and spent dismal evenings discussing the same weary question:

why? We were doing something perfectly legal, and had nothing to conceal. The government could only gain by helping us.

Claude Duthuit arrived from Paris, and his arrival changed our luck. A friend of a friend persuaded the president of the republic, Adnan Menderes, to intervene. We handed in the completed *Beyannami*, and that same night there was a riot at Istanbul University, where thousands of students were besieged by the army. Tosun and his student friends disappeared, we hoped not to jail, but were afraid to ask.

Later Tosun telephoned George from Ankara. His cousin had given him the name of someone in the American mission who was in charge of surplus, and would George be interested? George went to Ankara and obtained permission to salvage material from the American military junk piles in Turkey. I got on the next train, and found Ankara buzzing with revolution, though outwardly quiet. Big black Cadillacs of the Democrat party were cruising up and down Ataturk Boulevard, escorted by jeeploads of police.

George's new friend, Dan Siglin, was an engineer for the American water development project in Turkey. He gave us bourbon and fried chicken, and with a few phone calls arranged for us to be given legal free rein in the junkyards, from which we salvaged a whole mountain of material: a diesel air compressor, a generator, a hospital-size tent, welding outfit, pump, spare tires, shelter halves, jerry cans, tools, sheets, and even a jeep to carry it all away in, complete with an old set of Virginia license plates.

The final move from Istanbul was handled by a trucking company owned by Antalyans, pleasant men after our

weeks among the sour-faced Stamboulis. It was worth
going to their warehouse just to watch the Hamals, men
trained from boyhood to carry huge loads. The foreman
said his Hamals could carry up to five hundred pounds.

They had packs which built up the men's hips to allow loads to be laid across their backs at a forty-five-
degree angle, so that the weight was taken by their
knotty legs. They got good pay, for Turks, better than
three dollars a day. One little old man told me he wasn't
sure, but thought he was seventy, then walked off with
a whole truck engine on his back. His grandson held his
hand to steady him.

When they trotted up swaying planks onto trucks,
carrying their tremendous loads, I watched, fascinated,
waiting for one to fall. They never even stumbled. This
was not very original of me, since travelers in Turkey
had recorded their amazement since the early 1700's.

A telex came from Ankara. Our permit had been sent
via registered special delivery airmail. That night the
streets were full of tanks and armored cars, and the radio stopped broadcasting except for martial music and
periodic announcements of total curfew, with warnings
that anyone seen on the streets was liable to be shot. The
army had taken over the country.

The permit failed to arrive. We heard that all mail
from Ankara was being censored. Another copy was
sent by diplomatic pouch via the embassy. There were
rumors of fighting on the road to Izmir. The Aegean
coast had been a stronghold of the Democrat party and
Menderes, the deposed president, came from Aydin, the
dismal station between Izmir and Bodrum.

We went off for Bodrum in the jeep station wagon,
with George's old Eighth Army field jacket hung con-

spicuously over the back seat, and managed to arrive in
Izmir without incident. Often we passed safely through
roadblocks manned by grim-faced soldiers who held our
passes upside down for agonizing moments before waving us on, after a glance at the field jacket.

Mustafa and Rasim were entertaining Honor Frost,
Joan Taylor, and Frederic Dumas in Izmir, where we
had another windfall from the army surplus people:
mattresses, foot lockers, and more jerry cans. We
picked up Hakki Bey, who was assigned to represent the
Turkish government, and said good-by to Mustafa and
Rasim, who would not be able to join us except for a
week during the middle of the summer.

The loudspeakers in Bodrum hadn't stopped since I
left. Kemal was waiting for us in a cafe filled with the
wail of a *sark* from the radio and a recitation from the
Koran on the radio next door. I asked after his health.

"Fine," he answered, "and better now that you have
come, thanks be to God."

That same week the Minister of the Interior of the
defunct government, he who had been responsible for
torturing the students, jumped out of a high window
shouting, "Ya Allah!" The army arrested four hundred
and three members of parliament. And Captain Kemal
took off his cap to a man, the new military governor of
the district. He had been sent with a battalion to control
Bodrum.

Mandalinche had a new coat of paint, and her crew
was ready. Kemal had done well in finding us a diving
barge, a rotten old fifty-foot dragger named *Lufti Gelil*,
commanded by Kemal's friend Nazif Göymen, who
had served in the navy with him. Kemal had been only a

sailor, but Nazif had been first a diver and then the admiral's cook.

Later that night, when the women had gone to bed, we learned why Kemal had been disqualified from diving in the navy. It seems that they had all been asked to fill little bottles and Kemal just couldn't, not with all those others around.

"But I was scared," said Kemal. "In the navy when they tell you to do something, you do it. I looked around and saw a fellow who was peeing like a mountain stream, and got him to loan me a little . . ."

Nazif threw the punch line. "And ended up in the hospital!"

XVII

~~~~~

The Beach

THE TWO SMALL ships, loaded deep, headed for the
cape and the five islands which rose from the sea a
mile from it, where the wreck lay. Kemal knew a beach
which he thought would be a good camp site. It was
a deep indentation opposite a small island called Su
Ada, which Beaufort says was the Grambousa of Strabo
and the Dionesia of Scylax and Pliny. A mysterious
spring of fresh water gushes from it, although it is sepa-
rated from the mainland by a half mile of salt water a
hundred and seventy feet deep.

The cliffs rose sheer from the narrow patch of beach,
which was in most places less than fifty feet wide. We
found two springs under the cliffs, where generations of
voyagers had dug temporary basins in the sand to catch
the fresh water which seeped from the rock. The deep
bay, protected from all sides except the south, would
shelter us until fall when, said Kemal, "the south wind
will throw the waves up to there." He pointed halfway
up the high cliff.

As we stood talking on the deserted beach, a stone,

perhaps loosened by some small animal, came tumbling a hundred and fifty feet from the clifftop, and fell with a clatter on the pebble beach near us.

"It's a rotten place," said Kemal, "but the others are worse."

Nazif pointed to huge rock slides where the cliff had fallen a few years before. "When it rains, stones will fall, because the rain loosens the rock."

When we had unloaded the boats and camp building was well begun, we went out to the cape in *Mandalinche*. Captain Kemal held her over the spot under the jagged cliff where the wreck lay, and Dumas and I jumped over. I hung, adjusting my gear, under the boat. The water was clear, and the bottom was visible. My heart leapt when I saw the outline of the great boulder which marked one end of the wreck site. When we bottomed on the sandy patch in front of it, I saw the mark left on the rock by an ingot which we had prised up the year before. There was another nearby, in a place which I did not remember working in. Had the wreck been robbed?

We swam round, spotting green stains on the beach rock which marked hidden pieces of corroding metal. I searched for the place where I remembered a stone bowl. It was gone. In places where I remembered ingots from the year before, there was nothing. There were still ingots in the place which we were later to christen the "platform," but a stack of ingots which Mustafa had drawn in on the plan was gone. My air ran out. I pulled the reserve.

We hung the standard five minutes on the decompression stop, and surfaced feeling anxious. What if my estimate that there was at least a ton of metal were wrong? What if, as some of our detractors had suggested, these were only a few ingots dropped overboard by an overladen ship struggling to clear a passage between the islands? How would we explain this to the university and to our other sponsors? I felt better the next day when we found that many of the places which I had thought rock were really heaps of copper and bronze objects covered by sea growth.

During those first weeks of June we set the pattern which would guide our lives for the months to come. The problems of decompression from dives of ninety feet limited our safe diving time to sixty-eight minutes per day per diver — one dive of forty minutes in the morning, a second of twenty-eight in the afternoon, with six minutes of decompression for each dive.

Our first task was to define the outline of the wreck. Claude Duthuit and I made the first of many photographic mosaics of the wreck site, and Honor Frost laid out a first rough plan on the drawing board.

We slaved to build the camp. Nazif and Dumas drilled the rock where water seeped from the cliff, and everyone labored to build the catch basin. Copper and bronze from the wreck would have to be soaked for months, perhaps even years, before they could be dried out in the open air. Frederic Dumas found that he shared with Uncle Mehmet a passion for stone work, especially dam building. By the end of the second day, with Dumas in charge and Mehmet as assistant, a gang of "slaves" including George and Hakki Bey had dug out a pool behind the dam constructed by the water experts.

Dumas, in his spare time, built himself a "castle" at one end of the beach, with stone benches, a walk, and a

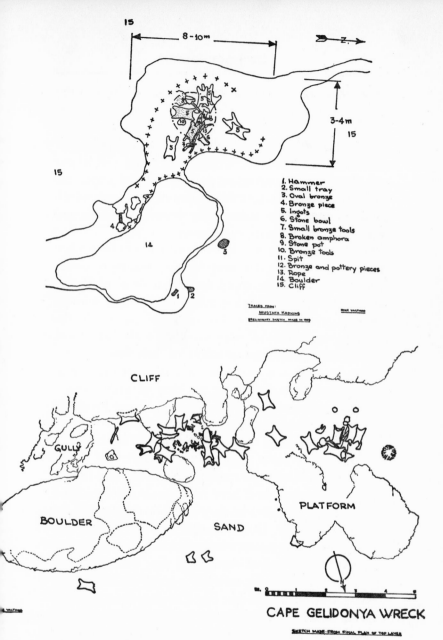

15

|← 8-10m →|

N →

1. Hammer
2. Small tray
3. Oval bronze
4. Bronze piece
5. Ingots
6. Stone bowl
7. Small bronze tools
8. Broken amphora
9. Stone pot
10. Bronze tools
11. Spit
12. Bronze and pottery pieces
13. Rope
14. Boulder
15. Cliff

3-4m

15

15

15

14

3

1 2

TRACED FROM:
MUSTAFA KAPKINS
PRELIMINARY SKETCH MADE IN 1959

MIKE VALPHONO

CLIFF

GULLY

BOULDER

SAND

PLATFORM

CAPE GELIDONYA WRECK

SKETCH MADE FROM FINAL PLAN OF TOP LAYER

The two drawings of the site clearly illustrate the difference between a survey sketch plan and a proper plan. It is remarkable that Mustafa was able to make a drawing so accurate while working under impossible conditions, alone, in 1959.

veranda. Herb Greer set up his darkroom in a cleft in
the rock. The generator that we had scrounged from the
dump heap ran perfectly from sundown till long after
midnight, when Herb finished developing and printing
the day's photographs.

We acquired a theme song. A magazine brought from
Istanbul had an account of the booming success of a
popular song that was sweeping America and which had
sold literally millions of records. Its title: "Itsy bitsy
teeny weeny yellow polka dot bikini." It was a great
day when we heard it sung for the first time over the
radio, and its effect when sung in chorus by Frederic
Dumas, Uncle Mehmet, and Herb Greer was indescribable.

The rotten tents salvaged from the junkyard sprouted
in clusters along the crescent of the beach. Nazif's
cook shack was at one end, and the main spring and
central camp in the middle, with the biggest tent attached by pitons to the cliff at its rear, and the front guy
ropes lashed to boulders in the sea. Here we lived,
worked, and slept. Toward the other end of the beach
we set up the compressors and the generator, so that
their noise would not drive everyone mad. "Dumas
Castle" rose on the heights at one side of the bay, beyond the generator shack, which was an ancient parachute stretched out like some medieval knight's pa-
vilion. We slept on the mattresses from Izmir, since the
budget wouldn't allow cots.

If the bowl of cliffs surrounding the bay assured us of
secure anchorage for our small ships and kept us from
being blown as far as Cyprus by the *meltem*, they also
caught the heat. The beach faced the rising sun, so that
a few minutes after sunrise it was so hot that it was an

effort to move. The fresh water bred mosquitoes which plagued us. The beach was not sand, but small stones the size of a man's fist or smaller. By ten o'clock in the morning they were too hot for even the Turkish sponge fishermen to walk on with bare feet.

In the early morning we drank tea, discussed the day's work, and loaded ourselves aboard *Lutfi Gelil* for the hour's run to the wreck site. By the second week we knew approximately what we were dealing with. The entire area of the wreck was about fifty feet by twenty. One side was delineated by the "cliffs," the bottom of the slope down which the ship had slid thirty-two centuries before, after striking the rock above. At the southern end of the wreck area was a great boulder. To the north the sandy bottom ran forty or fifty feet to a heap of rocks which was part of the cliff as it curved. In the middle of the wreck area was the "platform," a rocky shelf covered with ingots.

The shot line, down which we descended every day to the wreck, was attached to the cliff near the platform. If we hung on this line, twenty feet off the bottom, nothing seemed like a ship or any part of one. As we descended, bits of ingot became visible.

Kemal had borrowed two anchors from a friend who had found them in the sea a few years before. They should have been in a museum, and would have been, anywhere but Bodrum. Of forged iron, they were over eight feet long, four-pronged, with a very large ring at the end for attaching the great hemp cable of some seventeenth- or eighteenth-century galley. They were the largest grapnel anchors that I had ever seen.

Kemal hitched them to an old *kangawa* wire, dropped them over, and attached an oil drum for a mooring buoy. Then, in order to be securely moored, we had simply to pick up the buoy to which the descending line was also attached, take a turn with the wire around the bow cleats, run our stern line to the rock where the Bronze Age ship had struck, and lead the descending line to the diving ladder.

On the bottom, the wreck site soon began to look like a conventional archaeological excavation, with meter poles scattered everywhere and numbered plastic tags marking all visible objects. We plotted and photographed, with George forbidding us to raise anything until he was certain that the objects were drawn in place on the plan. Our familiarity with the area increased every day, and as we began to chip away at the rock that covered everything, we discovered more and more material in places that we had first thought were only rock. As we began to raise objects, we discovered interesting things about the concretion, and about the process of dissolution of the bronze itself in the sea. In some places the concretions had grown five to ten inches over the rock. We found that it was possible to free objects with hammer and chisel without breaking the object. But if the concretion were allowed to dry it became harder to free from the objects it covered.

Most of the bronze had retained its shape, but some was soft as cheese when wet, and when it dried became brittle like plaster. It was green-gray straight through. The good yellow metal was gone, dissolved into the water around it by electrolysis between bronze and copper, and between copper and tin. There were different rates of corrosion in different areas of the wreck. Was **this** because of variations in the alloys of the metal, or because of different rates of electrolysis in different parts of the wreck? The wreck was a fascinating problem from the chemist's point of view, but the answers to these specific problems will never be known, because Turkish law forbids export of any of the material, even small samples for chemical analysis, and we had been unable to find a chemist to analyze materials on the spot.

The year before, I had hoped that we would find that there was some wonderful new chemical process to clean the overgrown bronze pieces. But the experts whom Miss Taylor had asked all agreed that the best way in the circumstances was the most delicate possible version of the old "hit it with a hammer" technique. Only if permission could be obtained to export the material so that it could be treated in laboratories abroad would "magic" methods of cleaning be possible. Reduced to primitive cleaning methods, we spent our evenings with hammer and chisel, chipping limestone from the objects which had come up that day.

The current ran nearly every day, flattening the surface of the channel into a smooth river which only betrayed the force of its flow where the sea met the rock, and in the eddies which whirled around our buoys. It changed direction, sometimes in an hour or less, and some days ran faster than others. Captain Beaufort had also remarked the current: "We found it one day almost three miles an hour, and the next, without any assignable cause for such a change, not half that quantity . . ." He concluded that it would form an interesting subject for future investigation.

We confined ourselves to trying to find out how to work in it without getting in trouble. It was not bad once we actually arrived on the bottom, but getting down and up was sometimes difficult. A diver jumped over the side, careful to be near the shot rope that led to the wreck, because it was impossible on most days to swim in open water against the force of the current. Once on the line, we went down, hand over hand, our bodies flapping like flags. On the bottom we were protected by the basin in which the wreck lay, and in most areas of the wreck the current was slight.

We became blasé about the current. Not so the helmet divers. Kemal had come to Gelidonya with *Mandalinche* and his divers, prepared to work with us on the bottom when the current allowed. Although the current ran hard at least half the time, there were days when there was little or none.

We were cutting out ingots from the solid rock when Kiasim and I decided to try working together. He would swing the heavy sledge while I held the chisel. During the dive, the current increased, pulling his diving hose into a great curve. Surfacing, he lost his grip on the shot line and was swept away. We spotted him at the limit of the length of the hose, a hundred yards downstream from the boat. The boys pulled with a will to drag the helpless figure aboard. As he came alongside we heard a strange sound from inside the helmet, like the struggle of a lobster as he is dropped into boiling water. It was Kiasim, swearing.

When they twisted his helmet off, Kemal chided him gently for trying to go to Finike without leave. Kiasim, incoherent with rage, made the cliffs ring with his curses. For the rest of the summer we could always get a rise out of Kiasim by asking if he wanted to go to Finike, and "going to Finike" became our standard term for getting caught in the current.

Our commissioner, Hakki Bey, soon learned to dive,

and began to work with us, swimming like a happy whale in circles around the wreck. He was loved by the Bodrum men, and got along very well with the villagers who came to sell us garden produce. It was fitting that we should work together, as this excavation was certainly the product of his vision.

Trapped on the beach, however, we soon became weary of each other's company, and the trip to the wreck site was almost always spent in reading pocketbooks, some of which we had from the USIS library in Ankara. George and I began a beard-growing contest. As protection from the sun, Uncle Mehmet made a turban from a strip of old bedsheet. The rest of us wore turbans too.

The personalities of the new members of the Turkish crew came into focus. Nazif, the captain-cook, was a fine cook and a good mechanic, but a timid captain. His assistant, a boy from Bodrum named Jumhur, was an incurable pessimist in whom the Yok complex was developed to its maximum. Jumhur always looked at the weather and said, "It will storm." He looked at the boiling of the current and said, "Impossible to dive." When something broke, he would lean back with a comfortable sigh and remark, "It's broken." On the other hand, he was always willing to tackle anything. He attacked every job violently, without prior thought. Jumhur had the largest feet in proportion to his size that I ever remember having seen on a human being. They were horny, covered with thick tortoiselike layers of callus. I grew weary of the sight of him bounding joyously toward me over the burning stones of the beach to tell me that the compressor had quit again.

Besides Kiasim and my old friend Uncle Mehmet, who

had found the wreck, Kemal had brought a diver named Mustafa who was a good seaman but automatically went to sleep whenever he stopped moving. Diver Mustafa, a good and quiet deckhand named Mehmet, and a boy, Osman, were cousins from Dirmil village near Bodrum. Gunai, from Bodrum, persuaded George in Bodrum to hire him as Nazif's helper, and afterwards became a permanent member of George's group in Turkey.

By the end of the month we were well established. I wrote in my diary: "This is a battle. Our weapons are the stamina in our bodies and our ability to keep everything running and, most of all, our morale. We are pitted against the inevitable beginning of the *lodos* wind, which will wash us off the beach at the end of August or the beginning of September, and the fact, which is becoming more apparent every day, that the mechanical basis for our expedition is a collection of outmoded junk . . ."

Our greatest asset was perhaps the enthusiastic curiosity that had brought everyone to Gelidonya, which was even shared by the Turkish sailors. What was the ship like? What, really, were we going to find under all that beach rock? Gold cups? A treasure of Mycenean jewelry? Nothing?

XVIII

∾∾∾∾∾

The Lumps

THE HOT DAYS went on. We plotted and raised a continual succession of similar material, parts of ingots, broken bronze tools, and ballast stones. Our great hope was the heap of objects which formed the platform. For days we had discussed what should be done to it. Finally Dumas proposed that we break it off all in one piece after plotting its position. But how? Dumas remembered the hydraulic auto jack in the jeep back in Finike. We sent *Mandalinche* to get it, and Claude and Dumas went to work to chisel a hole underneath the lump so that it could be inserted.

George at first opposed the idea of the jack. Dumas and I argued that if we could raise big sections and put them together on the shore in exactly the way they had lain on the bottom, we would be able to reconstruct how the ingots had fallen when the ship sank. This would save a great deal of time, as the most time-consuming part of our whole job was triangulating ingots in place. Dumas and I labored under our experience, which had taught us that the prime problem was how to work fast without wasting diving time. George did not agree. His view of archaeology transcended anything we could say or do. Dumas' and my combined experience of diving came to at least thirty years, about the span of George Bass's lifetime. We argued on the basis of experience, of what we chose to call "knowledge." George infuriated us by violating the rules of efficient diving work on the bottom. When he came to a problem or question of whether the plan was correct, whether the material had been recorded in place thoroughly enough to permit its raising, George always stopped to check. He was capable of holding up the entire job for days, while he used up his diving time in mulling over how best to raise a small object. He was, of course, absolutely right. If we were attempting a correct archaeological excavation under water, then it was just that, and not a diving job in the ordinary sense of the term.

The jack idea was our first big compromise. It was good underwater practice, and we hoped it would also turn out to be good archaeology. Claude and Dumas dived and chipped under the northwest corner of the platform. By the end of the week they had a hole big enough to take the jack. Claude and I dived with it, got it under the mass, braced it with wooden blocks, and pumped. The jack tightened, but went no farther.

We surfaced, furious. When I got the jack apart, I discovered that salt water had leaked into it. We topped it up once again with oil, and handed it to Dumas. He dived alone, looking determined. In thirty-five minutes he reported the lump loose and ready for lifting.

Captain Kemal eased *Lutfi Gelil* over the wreck. Dumas dived again to shackle the lifting wire onto the lashings. Jumhur hove down on the stick that controlled the primitive winch's drive belt. The mast groaned as the weight came on it. The whole structure of the ship creaked and she heeled far over. The wire, stiff with strain, was bar-tight. Kemal shouted. All the men hove in unison on the big drive wheel of the winch. There was a jerk as the lump broke free.

For a moment it dragged on the bottom, and George gasped. It came free and the engine took the strain. The lump rose steadily. Everybody yelled when it broke the surface, swaying, green, mysterious, alongside *Lutfi Gelil*. Kemal ordered everybody away from the straining gear. He yelled, and bent to the drive wheel. The mass swung inboard clear of the bulwark. We laid it onto the tire that had been set on the deck for it to rest on.

What had seemed rock on the bottom was in reality cargo: broken bronze tools, bits of ingots, half and whole ingots, held together by limestone sea-growth. Guided by Dumas, who had a fine eye for possible weak points, we became lump-raising experts, able to spot instantly the places where pressure could be safely applied, and where the underlying rock would break to fit the jack. We never broke an object in raising it, because the corroding metal had formed a cushioning layer of green mush between any object and the rock that had formed over it. No one had ever seen anything like it. I began calling it glurkus. For lack of a better word, George called it glurkus too. We had learned discussions about "banded" glurkus (the stuff formed by alternating layers of corrosion product and white sea-growth) and bronze glurkus, the stuff formed by bronze, not nearly so soft as copper glurkus, the soft and mushy bright green stuff that usually surrounded the ingots. Miss Taylor formalized the term when she began referring to it as "Glorkus" in her notes. The camp echoed with the clink of hammers as enthusiastic workers used hammers and chisels on the lumps, knocking off layers of sea growth that were often a handspan thick.

One day a heap of ingots on the platform split in the middle, revealing ropes and part of a basket lying between two of the ingots. Claude Duthuit and Herb Greer dived to lash the basket lump to the winch cable, which was then hove in till the lump hung above the bottom, and stopped off so that the delicate material could be wrapped in a protecting sheet before being raised. *Lutfi Gelil's* old engine chose that moment to stop with a wheeze, leaving the precious lump hanging ten feet off the bottom with the divers hovering, waiting to follow it to the surface. Nazif cursed Jumhur, I cursed Nazif, George looked ominous, and Frederic Dumas looked disgusted. Jumhur leapt into the hold and cranked the engine while Nazif worked the feed valve. It wouldn't start. We turned the big winch flywheel by hand until the lump was up, everyone who could fit in the cramped space straining to do his part, Captain Kemal jumping and cheering us on.

The lump broke surface and with it came Claude and Herb, both furious. It seemed that Claude had had trouble in wrapping the lump with the sheet. Herb, torn between his desire to help and his photographer's instinct, had hung ten feet away, taking photographs, while Claude had pleaded with him in dumb show to come and help. George calmed them down and when they were coherent, they reported that where the lump had lain they thought they had seen planks.

This was confirmed the next day. There were bits of planking, and shadows of organic matter that showed where planking had rotted away. We had found, at last, part of the ship. George telegraphed the University Museum: TONS CARGO HULL MAYBE SAILS PRESERVED SEVERAL YEARS JOB.

The pond began to fill up with cargo. There were plowshares, picks, hoes, axes, adzes, mirrors, chisels, knives, ax adzes, a spade, a spit, something that we puzzled over until we decided it was a pruning hook; what might be broken-up bronze tripods; and unidentifiable bronze scrap, besides dozens of the typical copper ingots and ingot fragments. One of the most exciting things we found on the platform was a lump of whitish, very badly corroded metal, which was analyzed by Rasim at his factory in Izmir and found to be tin. As it was tin ore, it must have come from nearby.

All this material seemed evidence that our ship might have been owned or chartered by a smith working his way up the coast with a cargo of copper and the tin for smelting it into bronze. Perhaps he gave new tools for old, making his profit from the weight of the metal when he made a new ax or adze or hoe in return for two or three old ones. The basket had contained broken tools, and was what remained of the baskets full of broken tools that had been our smith's raw materials.

We were proud of the "junk man" theory. One night I explained it to Kemal. He lit a cigarette, took a long drag, and said, "Peter, this thing of yours about collecting a lot of useless junk doesn't bother me too much. After all, we are good friends."

He fixed me with that hard look he used when making a point in argument. "But collecting *junk* that's three thousand years old . . ." He sputtered. "That's . . . that's . . . *ridiculous!!*"

XIX

$\sim\sim\sim\sim\sim$

Fatigue

THE LAST week in June began with jubilation over
the lumps, and ended in exhaustion and despair.
The bad period began when Herb's regulator flooded,
and he had to free-escape, abandoning on the bottom
our revolutionary new camera case, the one especially
built for us by OFRS to take our Polaroid camera. A
minute or two after he surfaced, choking spectacularly,
we realized that the case was still on the bottom. It took
several minutes more before we remembered that the
case was almost perfectly balanced, neither positive nor
negative in buoyancy. The sun was warm and pleasant,
and I was cold after diving. There was no other diver
on the boat. One of the men ninety feet below would
surely spot it. No one did.

We spent the next two diving days searching for it, all
of us knowing that a search was hopeless, for if it had
been slightly positive we should have spotted it on the
surface. If negative, it must have gone to several hundred
feet and been crushed by the pressure soon after drifting
off the wreck site. We were determined to find the thing
anyhow, against all logic. Kemal and his divers searched

also, frightening me by staying down far over proper decompression times.

On the last dive of the search, Dumas surfaced with a sea turtle clutched in his arms. He had surprised it sleeping on the bottom. When we arrived in camp we drilled its shell near the tail, and attached it to a nylon line while we discussed what to do with it. The debate raged while the turtle swam to the end of the line and paddled seaward, apparently not noticing that it wasn't going anywhere. The camp immediately divided into two parties, the school of "eat the thing, we're hungry," and the opposition, led by Miss Taylor and supported by Herb and Honor, who said, "Let it go, poor dear, it's so cute."

Dinner was rice and beans, as usual. We had had no meat for a week. Dumas led off for our side with the story of a delicious turtle eaten somewhere in the Indian Ocean. I followed with a description of turtle steaks fried in butter in Honolulu. Our side lost a point when Miss Taylor forced us to admit that neither of us, personally, had ever butchered a turtle. George, bemused and neutral, sat listening to both sides. Claude Duthuit remained neutral. After dinner we carried the argument to Kemal. He confessed that he had never eaten a turtle, but was willing to take a chance. Uncle Mehmet supported our side.

"It's wonderful meat, good with raki." He looked around sinfully. "Like pork."

"Wonderful shish kebab," added Diver Mustafa.

Nazif, the captain-cook, settled it. "Everyone knows it's the worst kind of bad luck to kill a sea turtle." Jumhur nodded sagely. "Anyway," Nazif added, "I don't cook it."

George reluctantly said that he supposed we had bet-

ter let it go. When we went to release it the next afternoon, it was still swimming in place. Dumas and I watched
it swim away. My belly growled.

"Have a cigarette," said Dumas.

"Sublimate," said George, lighting it.

That night the big high-pressure compressor broke
down. It had been giving trouble for weeks. Kemal and I
had spent nearly every evening fixing small things, like
popped high-pressure fittings. It had been getting worse
of late, refusing to come up to the requisite 1800 or
2000 pounds per square inch needed for the aqualung
bottles, and emitting an ugly, untraceable clatter as it
ran.

Kemal and I were still working, woolly-headed with
exhaustion at three in the morning, when George, who
had not slept, came to give us cigarettes and ask how
we were doing. Everything depended on that compressor. Without it we had no expedition. All we had left
was the tiny portable compressor that I had used for
two years, which had never been very good and was
now a wreck, and which took two hours to fill one small
tank.

Our trouble was that the whole expedition was built
on a very shaky platform of improvised, broken-down,
or inadequate machinery, which only ran at the cost of
backbreaking labor by the semiskilled mechanics in the
crew, Kemal and me. Although we were both able to fix
and rig anything in the camp, we simply didn't know
what a master mechanic should know, and spent hours
tinkering at jobs that a real mechanic might have done in
as many minutes.

Now we were as tired as the machinery. The week
before, I had strained something and now I groaned

around like an old man. Kemal did not make me feel better when he remarked that half his friends ruptured themselves at thirty. What scared me was the weakening of my body with the approach of middle age. I had led an active life. Now I realized that there were things that I could not do because I was too old. I had always thought weak guts were a joke. Now I had to ask younger men to help.

George had found a mechanic in Antalya the week before when he had had trouble with the jeep. He gave everyone a day off while we went to Antalya in *Mandalinche* to ask his help. The trip took fifteen hours instead of six, because the engine kept breaking down. Midway, rolling in the swell with Nazif and Jumhur sweating over the engine, Kemal pointed to the shore.

"Eski Hisar [old city]."

George and I peered at the shore, where a little bay led to what might have been ruins. It was Tekrova, the ancient Phaeselis, where Beaufort had been startled by the damage to a sarcophagus on the shore wrought in only a year by the sea. The place faced south, like our camp. We never had time to visit it, which was a pity because Beaufort had described it thoroughly. It would have been interesting to compare it with his description. Phaeselis was full of history. Alexander had visited the place. But we were never to see it; at Gelidonya we had no time for the comparatively recent past.

Mercan, the boat which Tosun had used as a base for our sponge-diving adventures of the year before, was tied up, abandoned, in Antalya harbor. She had come down to Antalya on a fisheries project which had come to a halt because of some sterile intrigue resulting from the change of government. It was sad to see her, such a good boat, with rust streaks thick under the scupper holes, rotting until she could be decently condemned and Ahmet the Pimp or his friends could strip her.

The waterfront cafe in Antalya, where we sat to drink our morning tea, was a dream of coolness and quiet, with a stream of water running through it and little tables in deep green shade. Our peace was spoiled by Nazif, who came up with the local newspaper of three days before. With Kemal's help, I deciphered it: AMERICANS FIND TONS OF GOLD.

We were besieged by a band of idlers who wanted to hear all about it, and who walked away shaking their heads when I tried to explain that we were after knowledge of the past, not gold. We sat, too tired to move and full of *kayf*, watching a grandfather play with a small girl of about three, who was basking in the loving friendliness of the men who had dropped their backgammon to watch her. When she was taken off by an elder sister, the old men turned to their games with smiles. We headed for the machinist's.

The shop was in a noisy back street which one approached through the blacksmith's quarter of Antalya, where piratical-looking mechanics and their apprentices, ragged children with sunken cheeks, fixed trucks, banged the giant water pumps that moved the irrigation water for southern Turkey, and tinkered with tin lamps, stoves made from tin cans, castings, and broken Japanese flashlights.

We came to a door where a sign hung, rusted and weathered so that only AHIM USTA was still visible. There was no need for a sign. Ibrahim, master mechanic, "usta," was standing in the door in well-creased blue trousers and a fresh white shirt. He shouted at his assistants, a boy of about twelve, who looked like a Turkish Oliver Twist, and a starved young man of perhaps twenty, in filthy overalls. They rushed to clear dismantled machinery from the only two chairs in the place, and ran out for tea.

We wandered around while Ibrahim shouted orders to his helpers, now reinforced by a small boy of not more than eight, wearing a man's shirt with great holes in it which exposed the greenish skin of his potbelly. I looked through the inner door into the courtyard of what must have once been the house of a rich merchant. Three stories of balconied galleries ran around a courtyard which might have been a garden but which was now occupied by a huge heap of automotive junk: gears, broken springs, heaps of broken bolts, worn-out pistons, and carcasses of stripped engines. In a far corner, an old man and his son were chipping tombstones out of marble from Phaeselis. The high, hollow clink of their chisels rang on the stone, punctuating the general roar of the district and Ibrahim's shouts as he worked his men.

Beside the door, white and neat, were two white lambs munching on grass so green that it seemed artificial. The only clean thing in the shop, beside the lambs, was our rebuilt jeep engine.

Ibrahim began with the compressor. One of the boys pulled the starting rope. It failed to start. The starved boy handed him a screwdriver, with which he made a tiny adjustment. It started and ran perfectly.

We went to lunch. Has any poet sung of the delights of lunch to a diver on his free day? We ate three kinds of meat, and Kemal told me about Ibrahim, how he had been apprenticed at twelve, like the little boys all over Antalya, and that he was now owner of half a dozen taxicabs and a couple of houses, including the one his shop occupied.

It was fun to watch Ibrahim work. His fingernails were long, and he never touched a tool with his carefully manicured hands unless he had to, and would drop it to the floor as soon as he had finished using it. It would then be retrieved by the smallest of the boys. I asked him why he didn't clean the shop, or the courtyard of his house. After all, he was the best mechanic in Antalya.

He replied, "But people expect a shop to be dirty."

I visited a doctor, who demanded payment in advance, examined me, and pushed me out the door. He said he wasn't ready to operate yet, to come back when it got worse, and refused to tell me anything more.

I went to the museum to call on the director, who was not there. I sat on the tribune's seat from an ancient theater to wait, and was entertained by the guardian, who brought me coffee and told me about his experiences during the First World War in Jordan and Syria. The war for him had been a round of dysentery and dust. He had never heard of Lawrence of Arabia. The Arabs, for him, had been abstract dangers, like the wolves of the mountains of Anatolia, where he had never been.

He fell asleep beside me on the stone bench, his head resting on one of the stone dolphins which decorated its back. I dozed too, reflecting on a sarcophagus in the courtyard which was ornamented with a relief of wild-pig hunting, with the mountains where that man had hunted pigs so long ago looming beyond. All that remained of him was his sarcophagus, the mountains, and the pigs. There was no inscription. Mustafa Kapkin and Rasim hunted pigs every winter, leaving the carcasses to rot. I was dreaming of roast pork when the museum director arrived, and brought me back to Turkey.

XX

~~~~~~

The Narghile

WE MADE record time to camp, under sail and engine. Almost before the echoes of the anchor
chain running out had stopped bouncing off the baking
cliffs, we had the compressor set up and running. It ran
perfectly for twenty tanks, and then stopped. We tore
it down, found the trouble, and fixed it. It worked for
two days and quit. We found that a grain of sand had
scored a piston, and slaved over it for a whole day, gasping queasily for breath in the hot July sun.

The flies had multiplied because of the hot weather
and the filth piling up around the cookshack. I railed,
begged, and ordered Nazif to get rid of the garbage. He
just couldn't see the relationship between flies and garbage. The result was that we were awakened by flies in
the morning, and lived with them till sundown. They
made it hard to concentrate, for if you stayed still a moment they began to settle, seeking out places where
there was a little scratch, a tiny cut, or eyelids, nostrils,
and corners of mouths. One day I counted fourteen
gathered round a cut on my leg not much larger than a
matchhead, feeding greedily in an indecent circle.

As we became weaker, cuts which would normally heal quickly became infected and reinfected by flies, until they turned into running sores which stayed open for weeks. If you could keep the flies off, they would heal. But this was impossible, because bandages would not stick in salt water.

With continual breakdowns, it was impossible to go on running the whole diving operation on one compressor, and there was no working high-power air compressor nearer than Germany. In a normal country we could have sent a telegram to the manufacturer and had our compressor replaced in forty-eight hours, but in Turkey this was impossible.

George, Kemal, and I drank half a bottle of raki one evening, smoking cigarettes, and came up with an idea. We would adapt *Mandalinche*'s low-pressure diving compressor to work on a "narghile" or "hookah" system, in which the diver worked with an aqualung regulator strapped to his back, fed with air pumped from the surface through a hose, instead of from high-pressure air tanks strapped to the diver's back. It was the system we had used the year before with Tosun.

Kemal and I set off for Antalya in *Mandalinche* to machine the necessary parts. As soon as the boat was tied up, he and I walked up to the cafe. Once more I understood the raptures of the Bible and Koran over running water, for to us the place was a dream of ineffable luxury with its dirty tables and teetering chairs by the side of a little stream, in the green shade of a plane tree. There were no flies. The tea was hot and very sweet.

A big passenger ship was anchored off the harbor. It debouched hordes of improbable tourists in bright-colored shirts, hung with cameras, who stared curiously at the two bearded characters dressed in rags at the cafe table. I stared too, studying the camera-laden Americans and the English in their gray flannels, just as the village Turks of two years ago had stared at me, and for a moment the foreigners seemed completely unreal. It was inconceivable that I spoke the same language as they. It took an effort of will to rise and trudge up the hill to the mechanics' quarter.

We got back the next day with the device rigged. An air hose led from *Mandalinche*'s compressor to a volume tank perched on her foredeck. An air manifold, made from water pipes, led from the tank to the diving hose connection. When anchored in the bay, we attached the air hose to the volume tank, and one of our aqualung regulators to its other end.

Kemal, assisted by a gloomy Jumhur, mumbling that the thing would never work, lashed the thing to my back. With Kiasim tending the hose, I jumped over and swam down to the sandy bottom. The air came well. Now we would not have to run the failing compressor so much. We could use bottles only for photography, and when the current ran so hard that it dragged the diver by its pressure against the hose.

Claude sewed up canvas straps, using a photograph in a diving equipment manufacturer's brochure as a pattern, and we set about learning how to use the new equipment on the wreck. The only hose we had available was an ordinary garden hose which kinked. We discovered that when working on the bottom, a hose kink would usually open and give you air again if you swam ten feet straight up.

With the narghile running, Kemal, Kiasim, Uncle Mehmet and I fell back into the old pattern that we had

known the years before on *Mandalinche*. Kiasim and
Mehmet, the best tenders, sat on either side of the bow,
tending the hose when the divers were down. Kemal and
I would sit on the cabin top, half asleep with the pounding of the motor.

One day we began to discuss religion, and Kemal
asked me why I did not become a Moslem. I was shocked
to discover that I could hardly find any theological reason which made sense to both of us why I should not, or
what the difference was between our respective faiths.

Kemal said, "Of course, your book doesn't tell you
about djinns." We moved from the cabin top to the
bows, and with Kiasim and Mehmet nodding to verify
every word, he told me horrible stories about the djinns
that had driven his uncle crazy. They appeared at night
as beautiful naked girls. At first the old man tried to make
love to them. He couldn't. He was too old. He begged
them to go away but they refused, wriggling their lovely
white breasts and making indecent gestures. The old man
died that winter, raving mad.

I was about to ask how we could recruit some of those
djinns when the compressor stopped with a clatter of
ripping metal, and we rushed to get the divers to the
surface. We headed back to camp with short tempers:
another diving day lost. We anchored in the bay and
the crew went ashore, leaving only the three of us on
board. Kemal and Kiasim set to work to tear down the
compressor, Kiasim protesting the heat and Kemal the
urgency. Big horseflies buzzed round the steaming boat,
giving us minutes of anticipation before they bit.

I crawled wearily up to the bows to tinker with something, suddenly heard shouting, and looked up to see
Kiasim coming at me in a rush, Kemal behind him wav-

ing a heavy iron frying pan. I got between them before Kiasim managed to get the knife out of the leather loop where it hung at the front of the cabin. That evening Nazif had a fight with Jumhur, who came to Kemal and me at the compressor station, threatening to kill Nazif.

The flies woke me at dawn the next morning. I trudged around the camp, persuading the reluctant crew to go on board. At noon Kemal came out on the launch, bringing us our lunch — tomatoes and dry bread — and then even *Lutfi Gelil*'s engine would not start. Kemal raged at Jumhur, and at last it fired. We putted homeward at two knots, and halfway there Kemal beckoned me to the engine shack.

"Now listen, Peter, there are five different sounds in this engine, and they are all symptoms of trouble." He raised his finger didactically. "The first is like this." He cocked his head and sang in a falsetto voice, "Ping, ping, ping, ping. That one is nothing. Now the second sound is like this." His voice became a deep bass. "Bong, bong, bong, bong. That is not bad either. The third, bak-bak-bak-bak, is nothing much. Neither is the fourth, ting-ting, ting-ting, ting-ting. But the one that we have to worry about," said Kemal, lowering his voice in serious anxiety, "is that terrible woof woof, woof woof, woof woof."

Just then the engine went "woof woof" and stopped, leaving us drifting toward Cape Gelidonya in the lowering dusk. I laughed at Captain Kemal, dirty and disgusted, a big smear of oil on his forehead, his shirt ripped down the front, raising a finger again. "You see? It *was* the woof woof!"

The next day the current got worse, and we struggled to use the narghile, because it was imperative to save the filled bottles for days when it would be impossible to use the narghile at all.

The narghile diver in the current would grab the shot line and work his way down it hand over hand. When he reached the bottom, he would lash himself in place with a slip knot, his knife handy in case the hose kinked and the slip knot jammed. It sounds more dangerous than it was, because the current kept the hose stretched so that it could hardly kink. The big problem was the terrific drag on the rushing current against the hose, which pulled into a great curve behind the diver, trembled at the small of his back, humming and vibrating as the water hit it. We were frightened many times, especially when there was not enough air pressure in the volume tank on the surface to give sufficient air to struggle on.

Small fish hung out on the wreck site, where they found that our work dislodged edible worms. One grouper got very friendly and at last I got a picture of a grouper doing his "inspector" act, hanging over a draftsman's shoulder and watching his hand moving over the drawing.

One day three men appeared in a hired boat from Finike. They had come to dive, they said, having heard about us from Mustafa Kapkin in Izmir. Waldemar (Vlady) Illing was German, twenty-three, built like an ox, and had come with his own tanks and a small compressor. George invited them to stay. Vlady and Claude became inseparable. Vlady was one of the best skin divers I have ever seen. He could skin it ninety feet to the wreck site, swim around, shake hands and surface, smiling. He was very strong, and a good mechanic.

"Kick" Lacroix was a regular army sergeant with NATO in Izmir. He had been with Vlady in the years when Vlady had bummed along the Turkish coast spearing fish for a living.

With someone new to talk to, the whole camp cheered up. With visitors to impress, we made a show of setting up careful work schedules, writing down in the morning what had to be done that day. A typical work schedule from about that time, copied from my notebook, goes:

July 7   To be raised:
1) Pot base No. m 12
2) The lump at the mouth of the gully which Didi has been working on and which is now ready to be raised.
3) Area 5 on the Platform, small loose objects and broken concretions.
4) Loose ingots Nos 1 and 2
5) The broken concretions lying in s, from Didi's latest work on the lump at the mouth of the gully.
To search, raise and plot:
Claude and Walter, Area s
Clean weed in gully, search sand area and plot whatever is found.
Photographs to be taken:
Shoot gully, black and white and color. Bead lump on the platform. Make a vertical covering shot around s, black and white and color.
Dumas and Kick, set pitons in the gully so that it can be drawn accurately.
Etc, etc.

The compressor watch was easier now, with extra hands to help, and two men who were cheerful, not yet tired and irritable, brought new life to the camp.

The current kept us frightened. One day it ran too fast for the narghile, and I went over the side with a tank on. Dive over, I attempted to bring up a partly filled basket, overestimating my strength and underestimating its weight. Halfway up, my panting became uncontrollable. I tied the basket to the shot line and surfaced, exhausted. Arms and legs like jelly, I could hardly hang on to the diving ladder. When I felt better I went down the line to decompress, and hung shivering in the cold water, pondering my escape. I'd been close to passing out. A little more, and I would have drifted down with the current, unconscious, to be picked up or not.

Diving accidents, like that one, are almost never spectacular, but just the gradual mounting up of trivial things until they equal death. On another dive I became sick with fear for no reason, had a terrible headache, and had to force myself to stay down. I examined the compressor and found that the air filter hadn't been cleaned.

Diving was no more to us than riding a bicycle, but the danger of the little things surrounded us. The fact that incidents had begun to happen alarmed me, for it meant that I was becoming so weak that I was careless.

My weakness showed in other ways. I became irritable, and more difficult than I needed to be. I had my first argument with Kemal, after three years in which we had never quarreled.

Kemal had told me that we had fuel to last until the "day after tomorrow." This was because he had been misinformed by Kiasim. He came to me, after checking the tank himself, to say that the "day after tomorrow" meant two o'clock in the morning. George jumped on me, I jumped on Kemal, who jumped on Kiasim and then came back and jumped on me. The expedition stopped for a day while Kemal and Kiasim went off to Finike to buy diesel oil.

When Kemal got back he was still angry. We stopped talking for days and, hating each other, kept up our struggle with the mess of junk that we were too ignorant to fix. The big compressor got worse. Even our brilliant Antalya mechanic, Ibrahim, gave up and confessed that he could not understand what was wrong with it. There was not any one thing, just a long series of minor ailments. It was as if that particular machine didn't *want* to work.

One night Kemal put the screwdriver back into the toolbox after adjusting the engine carburetor for the fifth time that night, and for the first time in days grinned at me.

"Let me buy you a drink."

He sent Jumhur down the beach for the raki, and we sat till nearly dawn, discussing gremlins. We both agreed they must be djinns of some kind, Christian djinns.

The next time he went to Antalya he brought back a foul-smelling little leather bag, which he tied in an inconspicuous place under the compressor base. I debated for some time how to account for this item, which Kemal assured me was made from very efficacious and mysterious things and was fully worth the five dollars it had cost. I finally wrote down in the account sheet: "Exorcising djinns — $5.00."

A day or so later Miss Taylor, who was doing the weekly accounts, asked what I had written. I glanced over her shoulder, and for once was grateful for my illegible handwriting.

"Special attachment for the compressor," I replied. The thing ran beautifully for nearly a week.

We were worried by the reports in the local papers,

and by the conversations that Kemal and I had with the
locals in Antalya. They were convinced that we were
hiding tons of gold in the camp. Mysterious hunters appeared on the cliffs, turning away without replying to
our greetings. Then one day, when we were resting for
the afternoon dive, a boat came by the wreck site. She
was a big trawler type, and flew no flag. She circled us
twice, coming very close, so that there was danger of
her cutting the lines with which we were moored to the
island. Hard, sunburned faces peered at us over the
bulwarks. Turks? Greeks? I photographed the ship, not
bothering to take the camera from its underwater case.
They sheered off, full speed around the island, when they
saw the camera.

This was frightening. It was possible that she was only
a Greek trawler, poaching in these waters, who had come
to inspect us only out of curiosity. However, there was
a good chance that she was a spy for an enterprising salvage diver, come to mark the spot so that he could raid
it when we left. This incident, plus the very real possibility that we might not obtain a permit for the next
year, increased the tension under which we worked. It
seemed very likely that whatever we left behind would
be destroyed by those who would come after. They
would dig for gold, paying no attention to the delicate
bits of wood that were the most valuable thing in the
wreck. The copper scrap they found would be kept for
a while as a souvenir, then relegated to the junk heap.
Even if it ended up in a museum, it would have little
meaning out of context.

In the evenings when we had time to talk, Kemal's
reminiscences turned increasingly on Ab-I-Din, the

black diver. It was in these waters that Kemal had seen him make five dives in one day to forty fathoms, staying nearly a quarter of an hour each dive.

"The raki was getting him then," said Kemal. "He would still open the bottles with his finger pushing in the cork, or challenge you to keep your fist closed on a table while he pushed it open with one finger. But he wasn't what he once was . . ."

"He got old," said sailor Mehmet, joining the conversation for the first time since I had known him. He had been ship's boy when Ab-I-Din died. I went to bed and dreamed of Ab-I-Din, and all the other dead divers.

The next day was beautiful and calm. Kemal and I stayed in camp to fill extra tanks, and headed out later with *Mandalinche*. There was just enough breeze so that the sun did not hurt, but not enough to kick up a sea. The little ship pushed steadily past the cape with hardly any motion. Kemal lifted the old diving helmet off its nest of hose, and put it on the cabin top between us. He shouted to the boy to bring the tool bag.

His hard hands delicate on the old brass, he broke open the valve spring cover, removed the spring and ground the valve, while I held the tools and little parts so that they didn't slide with *Mandalinche*'s motion. When the valve turned smoothly in its seat, he soaked the whole assembly in oil and put it back together, adjusting the spring so that the tension would let out the right amount of air when the diver hit the head valve inside. If the spring tension was too weak, a jet of water would leak onto the diver's head; too strong, the diver would have to push too hard and too often to balance his buoyancy. The job was done with an air of reflective familiarity. I thought of all the lives that valve had held surety for, my own included, and of Kemal's, which would depend on it that day. He tightened the retaining ring and gave the helmet to Mehmet, who put it back in place on the coil of hose, with a canvas over it.

I handed Kemal a cigarette. He lit it with his lighter and handed it to me so that I could light mine.

"Peter Amja [uncle], we have a saying in Turkish . . ." He said something which I could not quite understand about a pot and a well. I paraphrased a half-remembered quotation into my bad Turkish.

"Do you mean that pots that go many times to the well are broken?"

He nodded. I said that we had that story in our book too, and for a while we were no longer Moslem and Christian, villager and educated city man, but men together in a boat on the sea, people of the Book.

Kemal said, "I'm going to quit, Peter. I have been diving for twenty-five years. Now I have a garden and a wife and beautiful children, thanks be to God. I am forty-two years old. When I was young, I brought two hundred and fifty kilos by myself in a year, and we dived deep in those days. I've spent ten minutes, fifteen minutes, in forty fathoms on the *manjura* boats for days on end, and laughed at it. Not now, not now. When a man passes forty . . ."

Kemal had been the lion of Bodrum, the man who never got bent and who had watched his friends killed or crippled one by one. We sat silent on the cabin top, watching the smiling sea and puffing on our cigarettes, until he grunted.

"The pot to the well . . ." he said, and made the old

brutal gesture used among divers in place of the word "death," it being bad luck to speak of death on board a diving boat. Right hand extended, palm up, he turned his hand over. Kemal stood and went to his customary solitary place in the bows, leaving me alone.

XXI

~~~~~

The Captain's Chest

WE LABORED to free the rest of the platform. Our excitement over the quantity of material that we were finding was deadened by fatigue and the miseries of life on the beach.

We now knew that we were dealing with the largest single find or "hoard" of Bronze Age metal ever found. By midsummer we had raised twenty ingots and pieces of more. Mixed with the mass of concreted copper and bronze on the platform were bits of pottery which dated the wreck definitely to the thirteenth century before Christ.

When we raised one of the last of the lumps from the platform, Claude Duthuit found under it half a broken pot filled with seashells. When it was plotted and raised, the "shells" were recognized as beads. Perhaps they had been a private trading venture of one of the crew, for the area in which they were found was almost certainly the forepart of the ship. There was jubilation at finding something different, something almost personal.

Herb Greer looked at them and cried, "I mean that's thrilling, thrilling, like mad, a gas . . ."

Dumas ran around gay as a sandpiper, saying "It's a gas, a gas, an archaeological gas! Let's count them!"

There were hundreds, all the same color, green and light green. Miss Taylor felt that they were Phoenician, and that they had been originally blue and white. They were very soft, collapsing if only a tiny bit of pressure was applied to them. They exploded into dust if allowed to dry out.

The next day we found the other half of the pot which had held the beads, and lying next to it a bronze bangle and a perfectly preserved double ax, its edges still sharp, the best-preserved tool we had found to date.

Dumas, looking slyly at George, stage-whispered, "I want that one for a souvenir."

Everyone laughed. The fact that no one could ever hope to have a souvenir was a sore point.

The lumps, cleaned and put back into place on the beach, showed how the hull had rotted and collapsed, leaving the cargo in a heap on the bottom, to lie undisturbed for three millenia. When we had finished the platform, we moved our lump-raising operations to the gully, following the traces of planking which ran under the rock. Little planking was preserved, but there was enough to show the line of the ship's hull, and neatly drilled auger holes could be seen in some of the wood fragments. There were no nails. The ship had been held together with wooden pegs.

Ann Bass arrived from America, and George brightened up considerably. Still, it was a poor place for a honeymoon. Nazif presented her with a pet rabbit, which she named John. He lived in the darkroom, and ate watermelon rind.

The gully area was full of material. Protected on the

one side by the great boulder and on the other by the cliff, the cargo was more in place there than on the exposed platform. We lifted a small lump at the very mouth of the gully, and exposed a solid mass of bronze tools and delicate organic matter. We tackled it with great care, working barefoot, so that the wash set up by a badly placed swim fin would not displace the delicate material.

On the first day something gleamed white, big as a fingernail, in the sand. It was a scarab, the Egyptian cartouche still sharp and clear on its underside. The next day we found a stone mace head, a bit of rotted wood still in its shaft hole, with a thin copper covering over it.

The organic matter at the mouth of the gully might almost have been a disintegrated chest. We speculated that we had struck the captain's personal sea chest, and became even more convinced when we discovered scale weights of meteoric stone.

The area at the mouth of the gully and at that end of the boulder was covered with a heavy layer of sand. We set out to air-lift it, using the long tube of steel pipe which took compressed air into its bottom and spouted air mixed with sand through a filter into the water thirty feet above, exposing the rock which lay underneath the wreck. There Waldemar Illing found more weights and then, a wonderful discovery, a beautifully carved cylinder seal of hard black stone. It was a signature seal for sealing clay tablets. It was inscribed with three figures. In the middle was a deity wearing a strange tall crown on his head, with a worshipper on either side of him. Although further study has shown the seal to be from northern Syria, and five hundred years older than the wreck, we thought at the time that it was contemporary and that it might be Hittite.

This set us off on a round of speculation about the possible origins of the ship. We knew that the wreck could be reliably dated within a hundred years of 1300 B.C. (Later study of the material has shown that she went down about 1200 B.C.) We also knew that Rameses III, after the Battle of Kadesh, signed a treaty of nonaggression with Hattusilis III, King of the Hittites. Could it be possible that our cargo of copper and bronze was a tribute for Rameses, that our ship was carrying a Hittite tax collector, amassing metal to send to Egypt? The theory fell apart when we failed to find anything in the wreck that was definitely Hittite, but led at the time to wild conjectures.

We became more and more excited as we dug into the gully area. Major pieces of wood began to show up. They seemed to be ribs, running laterally across the presumed line of the hull. The wood was soft, but often looked almost new. If allowed to dry, it shriveled to a tenth of its original size. When we raised bits of wood they were put into plastic bags on the bottom, so that they never dried out and the problem of preserving them could be put off for a more leisurely time. As each piece of wood was uncovered, we pinned a numbered plastic tag to it and hurried to draw and photograph it in place before the current washed it away.

The area of the gully was not large, perhaps the size of an ordinary double bed, slightly narrowed at the end away from the platform. As we moved into the "foot" of the bed, we found more personal objects: three more scarabs, a lamp, a bronze bracelet, and more hematite weights, until we finally had three complete sets of weights. Two sets were round, the bottom flattened so that they would not roll, the third shaped like tiny footballs flattened at one side. The smallest of them was little larger than a pea, the largest slightly smaller than a golf ball. Altogether there were fifty of them. When George studied them a year later, he found that they would have allowed the ship to trade anywhere in the eastern Mediterranean: Troy, Cyprus, Syria, Palestine, Egypt, Crete, and possibly Greece. They were far more accurate than anyone had previously believed possible for the Bronze Age. Twenty-six of the fifty are accurate to less than one hundredth of a gram.

Personal objects continued to appear: a piece of rock crystal as long as my forefinger, another mace, a finely carved whetstone. We hung the big air lift in front of the gully and lifted the sand out that was swept from the gully's mouth by the diggers, waving their hands as fans to move the sand. It rumbled and boomed. Compressed air was fed into its mouth through a valve which could be controlled by the divers, forcing sand up to the catch bag thirty feet above. The surface of the pipe was ice cold when it was working, and the air that bubbled out was also cold. It would have been wonderful for cooling beer, if we had had any beer.

Although we drew and photographed everything very systematically, we could make little sense out of the positions of the objects at the gully's mouth. They obviously belonged together, but had been scrambled by the collapse of the hull, which must have hung between the gully and the cliff. Then as the wood rotted, its collapse must have scrambled the objects in the "captain's cabin."

Halfway into the "bed" we were confronted with a layer, several feet thick, of what seemed to be a section of the hull with its cargo in place. At the bottom were planks. Above them was a layer of sticks as big around as a man's finger, some cut at each end with one swipe of an ax. They could not, we thought, form an integral part of the hull of the ship, for the bark was still on. Above the sticks was a solid mass of cargo: rolls of cop-

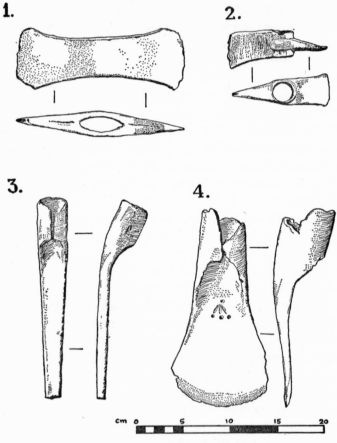

TOOLS FROM THE BRONZE WRECK
1. Double ax   2. Ax adze
3. Pick   4. Hoe or shovel

per sheeting, blank blades for making bronze tools, the sockets not yet shaped and unsharpened; and whetstones, not so nicely shaped as the "captain's." In the middle was a heavy timber which we were convinced was part of the ship's keel.

The sticks bothered us. What were they? Firewood, like the firewood *Mandalinche* carried? Not under the cargo, certainly. A day or two after we found them, I remembered something in the *Odyssey*. I picked up E. V. Rieu's translation and turned to the place where Odysseus built his boat or raft on Calypso's island:

"First she [Calypso] gave him a great axe of bronze. Its double blade was sharpened well . . ." We had found several bronze double axes in the wreck, one with well-sharpened blades. "Next she handed him an adze . . . Presently Calypso brought him augers. With these he drilled through all the planks . . ." There were auger holes in the planks we had found, and they too had been fastened with dowels. Finally, Odysseus was completing the ship:

"From stem to stern he fenced her sides with plaited osier twigs and a plentiful backing of brushwood . . ."

When, at the end of the summer, George studied the passage in Greek, he found that it had always been a problem for translators, because the scholars did not understand the purpose of the brushwood. We knew now, twenty-seven centuries after the saga of Odysseus's wanderings were written down, thirty-two centuries after those wanderings were supposed to have taken place. The brushwood was to make a bed for crew and cargo, so that the thin planks would be protected from inside. This would make inner sheathing unnecessary. Additional proof of this was given when the sticks were studied by an expert. They were a kind of brush common in Cyprus, where the ship picked up her cargo of copper ingots.

There was a quality of wonder about the wreck that never left us. I especially remember one dive of about that time. Eric Ryan, an assistant professor of art history at Colgate, had come out as draftsman and he and I made a narghile dive together, trying out a new system he and George had worked out. One excavator worked while the draftsman stood by to draw objects as they appeared. It was very calm and clear, and there was no current to plague us. At the head of the gully, under the ingot where I had found the first scarab, there was a group of new pieces of plank. I gently swept the sand, removing them and putting them in plastic bags when Eric nodded. In the middle of the wood there was a scarab. Just before coming up I glanced at the packed sand by the ingot, stained green by the leaching of the copper, and saw a second scarab and two weights.

When we surfaced I sat on the breasthooks in the bows of *Mandalinche*, where I had sat so many times, and jotted my notes, fighting to write legibly against the vibration of the one-cylinder engine. Finally I gave up and looked at the slate-colored sea and the gray lumps of the five islands melting together in the twilight. The great cape of Gelidonya, abeam of us, sloped back into the sea, which sparkled with the last of the sun.

I thought of those mysterious mariners and their ship. Who were they? What did she look like? They had looked at the same scene, very much as I was seeing it now. They, and how many others? Some I knew — Strabo and Beaufort and Scylax the younger. However inaccurately, I could visualize them, and should we meet,

I would not be at a loss for conversation. But when I looked at the box on the foredeck which contained the things we had raised that day, the scarabs invisible in their plastic bags; parts of an ingot broken three milleniums ago by a smith to forge into a tool which he was never to make; the planks in their plastic bags; the personal possessions of the crew and the cargo of their ship, which was now taking its next to last and shortest voyage from the bottom of the cliff where the wreck lay to our camp I thought that surely we and our machinery would be unimaginable to those men, who would have recognized the islands and the cape immediately, but, unlike Strabo or Beaufort of Scylax, would find the jump from their time to ours, their life to ours, inconceivable. For they lived at the dawn of western civilization, and we in the twilight of it.

XXII

~~~~~

The Hull Lump

WE DECIDED that it would be extremely difficult, if not impossible, to excavate the "hull lump" on the bottom. Unlike the lumps of cargo that we had raised previously, it was made up of fragile organic material. The only way to remove it in one piece was to cut under the bed of rock on which it lay. Doing this was going to be very difficult indeed, because it meant cutting the whole thing out of the living rock, which was like marble.

The area to be cut was three feet long by two feet high by three feet deep. We had thought of buying a jackhammer when setting up the expedition, but had decided to use the money for something more immediately necessary. Now we were faced with the prospect of making that big cut in hard stone, under ninety feet of water, with hammers and chisels.

To make things worse, we were exhausted, and were losing our best divers. Frederic Dumas' leave was almost over. Waldemar Illing, our steady German diver, got a letter from his family demanding the return of the truck that he had driven to Turkey. He decided to leave immediately, promising to return in a few weeks. Then we were struck by an epidemic of dysentery, caused by the filth and flies on the beach, but prolonged by malnutrition. Kemal fell into a state of total despondency.

The Department of Antiquities in Ankara wrote George ordering that the material from the wreck be shipped immediately to Izmir. Kemal swore that if this happened he would guarantee five thousand signatures on a petition from the people of Bodrum. We wanted the material kept there so the divers might profit by it, and learn the value of keeping antiquities.

We were out of food, out of fuel, out of money, and were running out of time. Kiasim forgot to put oil in *Mandalinche*'s engine, and it froze up solid. Kemal threw him overboard. The old man swam ashore, and for days skulked out of sight of Kemal, mumbling threats.

Seton Lloyd, director of the British School of Archaeology in Ankara, arrived with his wife. The day they went out with *Lutfi Gelil*, Nazif smashed his hand while mooring to the buoy over the wreck. Gunai, the cook boy, was bitten on the chest by a monstrous scorpion. He recovered rapidly after watching George and me fumble with the antivenin serum, our incompetence obvious to everyone.

There were bright spots. Dan Siglin, our engineer friend from Ankara, turned up with cases of canned food and magazines and fixed the generator for us. Anne Bass cheered up George, and through George the whole camp. Her presence smoothed things out somehow, and when she saw to it that George was provided with clean shirts, the rest of us washed ours.

Our worst problem was food. The villages nearby did not have enough to spare to feed so many extra people.

Claude Duthuit was absolutely shattered one day by a full-page color photograph, indecently realistic, in one of the women's magazines brought by Dan Siglin's wife for Ann Bass. It showed a succulent steak surrounded by vegetables and fried potatoes. He tore the page out, and there was a rumor that he kept it under his pillow.

Uncle Mehmet and sleepy diver Mustafa conspired to steal John, the rabbit, and eat him. They were betrayed by Jumhur to Nazif, who lectured them so severely that they set off on a mad expedition to pick flowers for Ann. They gave it up after Mustafa fell off the cliff.

As a pretty woman among a band of wild men who hadn't seen a woman in months, Ann managed to bring out everyone's protective instincts. Trained as a musician, she alone had no ax to grind. Her only reason for being there was George. It could well be argued that Su Ada beach was no place for a honeymoon, but on the other hand, if it's right to begin a marriage by learning about one's partner, she was doing just that. George was certainly going through the toughest period of his life, haunted as he was by the disintegration of his crew's health, our lack of funds, and the specter of looting which would almost certainly follow our departure. George collapsed from a combination of exhaustion, dysentery, and nervous strain, and was nursed by Ann and Claude Duthuit, who was a good man with a hypodermic needle.

Miss Taylor's promised draftsman and photographer team arrived and took over a large part of the demanding job of recording every single object we found. The photographer, Peter Dorrell, had worked for Miss Kenyon at Jericho. Terry Ball had come to archaeological excavations for years, trading his skill as a draftsman for

weeks or months in return for transportation to the excavation, his keep, and pocket money, as a relief from
life in England. He rigged a mosquito net to keep off the
flies and spent his day crouched under it, making drawings that showed objects better than any photograph.

We ran a shot line to the mouth of the gully, and
began cutting out the hull lump with sledgehammers,
working in teams of two. One man held the chisel; the
other swung the hammer. This took more skill than one
would think. It was not easy to stand in the current and
swing a heavy hammer so that it hit hard and true, knowing that if you missed you could break the chisel man's
arm. The helmet divers helped, but not often, never more
than two days a week. They had to struggle to keep on
their feet when we, with tanks, were unaware of the
current. When diving became difficult for us, it had long
since been rendered impossible for them.

At the end of the first week of work on the lump we
seemed no nearer to the end of the job. The "marble"
resisted us implacably. If we managed to cut into it one
inch in a dive, we had done well. Slowly, imperceptibly,
the lump became smaller as we worked on it. It was difficult to avoid touching it, and after a protruding piece of
wood had been touched enough times, it broke off.
George, desperate, decided to excavate it as it sat. I held
out for raising in one piece. George gave me another
week to work on the cut and we kept at it, worried about
the bits of wood which had been loosened by the shock
of the hammer and were washing away with the current.

Waldemar Illing came back from Germany with a
boxful of spare parts for the ailing high-pressure compressor, after having spent a week at the factory learning
fine points of its operation. We all retired into little

worlds of our own. Claude Duthuit and Waldemar Illing, the dashing Frenchman and the solid German, became inseparable. Ann Bass doled out pills. When anyone seemed to be dragging abnormally, big doses of vitamins seemed to pep most people up, especially the Turks, who were not used to any kind of medicine so that even aspirin had more effect on them than on the Europeans.

Though we were completely familiar with the wreck site by now, and hardened to the dullness of routine, fatigue, mechanical failure, and short tempers, from time to time we realized again the wonder of the mysterious world we had penetrated. One afternoon I was left alone on the site. I hurried to use the last minutes of precious time in cleaning marble chips from under the hull lump. The tools — hammers and chisels, a sledgehammer and a crowbar — lay in their places in boxes on the platform and by the mouth of the gully. The clouds of "dust" raised by our work were settling. The larger fish were beginning hesitantly to come back to the site.

It seemed very dark. As I moved to the shot line I thought that it must be dusk on the surface, for the water in the Mediterranean and Pacific seems to hold the light for an appreciable twilight time after the sun goes down. It is as if the sea had a quality of its own enabling it to hold light longer than air.

My hand was on the shot line when I heard a weird song going on all around me. I stopped moving and listened. Something chirped like a cricket, but trilling, louder and sweeter. I held my breath to hear better. I had heard the sound before, but where, how, in another life or merely in another world? The sound rose to a crescendo and stopped as I took a breath and moved a little up the shot line. It began again when I stopped and held my breath. It was not like the occasional chirpings one hears on a coral reef, but a pleasantly pitched baritone going steadily *Brruuup, bruuup.*

I started when a big pelagic grouper flashed across the wreck site, chasing a smaller fish. This was hunting time for the fish. I looked nervously around, keyed up for a possible dark shape looming in the semidarkness to attack, and end my speculations. The "telegraph," an iron bar put over the side of the boat and beaten with a hammer, signaled that diving time was finished and tapped me up the short line. I pulled my reserve and moved upwards, glancing at the bottom, at the tools which were resting in their normal places but now seemed to have aged suddenly, as if dissolved into their original elements by the inevitable sea. I hung for a strange six minutes on the shot rope, imagining all sorts of things. On deck I mentioned the singing. No one believed me.

XXIII

∽∽∽∽

Lodos

CLAUDE DUTHUIT turned the pages of the 1960 FOOD edition of an American women's magazine. He had arrived at the dessert section.

"Ah, the romance, the mystery, the excitement of underwater archaeology!" He handed me the open magazine and I flung it down. We had long since stopped talking about women, home, indeed anything but food and the lump which we had been slaving on for weeks.

Nixon Griffis, one of the members of the "board" which had made our expedition possible, had come from New York the week before to spend his vacation diving with us. He sat quietly nearby, observing the scene with the studied air of an anthropologist among aborigines. He had been diving twice a day, holding the bar for my sledgehammer as we burrowed under the interminable lump.

Claude collected his magazine and unwrapped his guitar to play "John Henry," the song of the "steel drivin' man, who laid down his hammer and died, Lawd, Lawd, who laid down his hammer and died." Griffis rubbed the dark bump on his hand where I had hit him with a sledgehammer.

George came out of the "drafting office," a packing box with the drawing board on it in one corner of the tent, and sat down on the sand with us. He and I had had a big argument in public the week before, an argument which had been so stupid and ugly that everyone had been particularly polite since then. The quarrel had, in its fashion, cleared the air. Now nothing concerned us but endurance. We had come a long way since that January day we had met in New York.

We talked of all manner of things, and finished with a bull session about the army. It was interesting that all of us had been in the army, Peter Dorrell, the photographer, in Palestine during the war; George and I in the Far East. Of the whole crew only Nazif and Kemal had been in the navy.

We broke up to go to bed. As I was pulling the sheet over my head to keep off the mosquitoes, a wave broke over me, followed by another. We piled out of bed and dragged our gear to the cliff edge of the beach. There was not a breath of wind. We had everything under control by two in the morning, recognizing the beginning of the *lodos*, the southerly gales of autumn which would cause great waves to break on the cliff itself and utterly destroy any camp on the beach. We spent the next day building a platform on the rockslide and moving everything but the most essential gear up onto it. We dug out the carefully arranged piles of ingots, excavating them from under two feet of sand.

Kemal said that a bad *lodos* would bring rain, which could loosen the rocks of the cliff looming above us. We raced to cut loose the hull lump, last and most important of all the lumps we had raised. We were haunted by the image of great waves smashing the camp while landslides fell from above to crush anything which had survived them.

Driven by this knowledge that we were about to be washed off the beach, and that if we left anything behind us it would not survive the inevitable looters, we worked like madmen and forgot everything except the job. Miraculously, everything functioned. The weakest divers among us worked as effectively as the strongest had at the beginning of the summer. Tied to the rock so that the current could not sweep us away, held down by forty pounds of lead, we swung the sledgehammer, sometimes striking the hand of the chisel holder as well as the chisel.

Some days the rock refused to crack. Sometimes we did three days' work during one dive, the rock splintering and falling away as the cut deepened. It was a great day when the lump, reduced in size but still nearly a yard square, the only surviving intact piece of a Bronze Age Aegean ship, trembled and broke loose. We lowered a wooden box to the bottom, slipped the hull lump into it, raised it, molded it in plaster, and then packed it carefully so that it could not dry out.

With an eye on the weather we searched the wreck area for material that we might have missed. Luis Marden of the National Geographic Society appeared with an underwater metal detector which he had managed to borrow. We swept the area and found a few deposits of broken tools and a bronze swage block, which had been used for drawing bronze wire. This was an important find, for it added to the evidence that the ship had carried a metalworker.

A week after Marden's arrival a steady wind began
to blow from the south. Kemal squinted at the sky and
turned to George.

"That's the *lodos*."

We packed up and loaded all the gear on the two
diving boats, wrapping the ingots carefully in sacks in
Lutfi Gelil's hold. The smaller tools we packed in plastic
bags in boxes, so that they would stay wet until we could
build a tank for them in Bodrum. The wreck site looked
naked. Great chunks had been torn out of the bottom,
and an area thirty feet long by ten feet wide was stripped
bare of weed and sand.

Kemal and I were the last to leave the beach, where a
boatload of local fishermen were collecting the debris of
our stay. The *lodos* that winter washed all the rest
away: tons of concreted rock chipped from the ingots
and tools, rock stained with greenish copper from its
thirty-two hundred years of contact with the metal.

On my last trip to Bodrum I met Uncle Mehmet,
original discoverer of the wreck. He told me with some
pride that the water tank still stands, and the Bodrum
boats always stop there for water.

Epilogue

As with any archaeological excavation, the story of
the Gelidonya wreck was only beginning when we
packed up our tools and left the site. The preliminary
reports have now been published (see Bibliography) and
we are at work on final publication of the material.
George Bass summarized the preliminary conclusions in
his report to the American Philosophical Society, one
of our sponsors.

"The cargo contained just over a ton of copper and
bronze tools and ingots, the largest and most important
such hoard discovered by preclassical archaeologists."

Space will not permit reprinting the full report, but
a paraphrased abstract gives an idea of its content:

Forty ingots of the oxhide type . . . Twenty-seven
of these bear what are probably foundry marks in the
undeciphered Cypro-Minoan script. Also found was
about twenty-five pounds of tin oxide.

Several hundred bronze tools, weapons, and household utensils were found, including axes, adzes, hoes, picks, a spade, hammers, chisels, knives, spear- and arrow-heads, bowls, a cooking spit, a mirror, and awls.

The theory that the ship carried a tinker is strengthened by several found objects, a bronze swage block like those still in use by metalworkers, a pair of perforated stone hammers, and a large, almost flat stone which might have been an anvil. Whetstones were also found. Whether the ship carried a smith or not, it was certainly a merchantman, since 48 weights were found, forming three sets. One set has as its standard the *qedet*, an Egyptian standard of 9.3 grams, used also in Syria and Cyprus. The standards of the other sets are not yet known.

Hammers, whetstones, and weights were found in the wreck area called the "captain's quarters." Here also were found four scarabs, including types found commonly in Palestine and at Byblos in Syria, a scarab-shaped plaque, and a finely carved cylinder seal probably carved in North Syria during the eighteenth or seventeenth century B.C. Here also were found the only lamp on board and traces of a meal: olive pits, fishbones, and bones possibly of a bird. An astragal for playing knucklebones was also found here.

Pottery dates the ship to the end of the thirteenth century, and has parallels in Cyprus, Syria, Palestine, southern Turkey, and Greece. Other items such as the seal, beads, and scarabs point to the eastern coast of the Mediterranean. All that may be definitely said now is that the ship was sailing west from Cyprus with a load of copper and bronze from that island. Among the 302 recognizable pieces of bronze, 232 are Cypriot in style, several of the letters found on these pieces are in the

Cypro-Minoan script, and the copper ingots are almost certainly from the copper mines in Cyprus.*

The dream of a museum of underwater archaeology in Bodrum has come true as this book goes to press. The Turkish government had appointed Haluk Elbe permanent director of the museum, and he has done a magnificent job of restoring the castle and building a small museum just outside the Knights' Hall, where visitors can see the finds from Gelidonya and the globe-amphora wreck at Yassi Ada, which George Bass excavated in 1961, 1962, and 1963. When the museum in the castle is completed, the bronze Demeter will be returned to Bodrum from Izmir, along with another statue found in 1962 by Bodrum sponge draggers.

When I last returned to Bodrum in the spring of 1963 I was told that there are now about 75 small boats, employing some 600 divers, all modeled after *Timurhane* and using the methods of narghile sponge-diving that we developed in the fall of 1959. Tosun Sezen has now fitted out the first Turkish sponge boat to make the trip to Africa.

Captain Kemal has retired from sponge diving to become George Bass's foreman, but still owns *Mandalinche*, which he has turned over to Kiasim and Uncle Mehmet.

Wreck III at Yassi Ada proved as interesting as we hoped it would. Enough of the hull was intact so that it will probably be possible to make a valid reconstruction of the hull on paper. In the cabin area, the diggers found a wealth of material, along with six gold coins of Heraclius (610–641 A.D.), which date the wreck. The cabin also contained what is probably the largest dated

* Abstract from Year Book of the American Philosophical Society, 1961, George F. Bass, pp. 459-462.

collection of pottery of this period: fifteen lamps, pitchers, a pipette for drawing wine from amphoras, many
cooking pots, and two bronze steelyards, one inscribed
"George the Elder, Senior Sea Captain." But that is
George Bass's story.

~~~~~~

Selected Bibliography and Notes

I HAVE given most of the sources for information in the book. No attempt has been made to give a full bibliography of material concerning underwater archaeology, or archaeology of Caria and Lycia. The annotations are made with the nonspecialist reader in mind.

As the book is an account of a personal adventure and very definitely not a treatise on history or archaeology, it has not been possible to include in the text background material and technical information which might be of interest to many readers, and without which a full understanding of our work is not possible. Such references are given below and should be available in any large library. I especially recommend to the reader the various technical articles about Gelidonya and Yassi Ada.

I am indebted to the British School of Archaeology in Athens and to the American School of Classical Studies for allowing me to use their respective libraries.

CHAPTER I

Francis Beaufort, *Karamania*, or a brief description of the South Coast of Asia Minor and of the Remains of Antiquity with plans and views collected during a survey of that coast, under the orders of the Lords Commissioners of the Admiralty, in the years 1811 and 1812. London, 1818.

A classic of its kind, full of information about the coast. Beaufort was a classical scholar as well as a seaman, and had a good ear for anecdote.

Beaufort recommended that the British government establish a consulate in Kos, across the straits from Bodrum. This was done. Charles Newton, onetime consul in Kos, led a big expedition to Bodrum, sponsored by the British government, in the 1850's.

Halicarnassos Knidos and Branchidae, published in London in 1862, is Newton's report on his excavation of the Mausoleum and is a mine of information. The bibliography contains everything written up to that time about Bodrum. The appendix to Volume II has a very complete description of Bodrum castle by Pullan, Newton's surveyor. Newton's "popular" book, *Travels and Discoveries in the Levant*, was published in London in 1865.

CHAPTER III

The Antikythera wreck: Unfortunately the source material on Antikythera has never been translated from Greek. The preliminary report was published in *Efimeris Arkhaologiké*, the journal of the Greek Archaeological Society, in 1902. This publication contains photographs of the statues before cleaning and of other material found in the wreck. An expanded account was published by J. Svoronos in *Ethnikon Mouseon* (Athens, 1906), from which one of the few accounts of the Antikythera wreck in English was taken: "Art Salvaged from the Sea," by G. Karo, *Archaeology*, I, 1948.

The best account of Mahdia is in *Visiteurs de la Mer*, Guy de Frondeville (Le Centurion, Paris, 1956). James Dugan's *Man Under the Sea* (Penguin Books, 1960) contains further information on Mahdia, with a bibliography.

Karo discusses Artemision. Professor Bean's account of his discovery of the Demeter statue on the beach is given in the *Illustrated London News* of November 7, 1953.

Underwater excavations: James Dugan in *Man Under the Sea* gives a good summary of work done in underwater archaeology up to the mid-1950's. A full bibliography of the underwater work done in France and Italy is given in Professor Fernand Benoit's final archaeological publication of the Grand Congloue wreck, *L'Épave du Grand Congloue à Marseille*, XIV, supplement to Gallia, C.N.R.S. (Paris, 1961).

Work not covered by Benoit in *L'Épave* has mostly been published in the *Atti Del II Congresso Internationali di Archeologia Sottomarina Albenga 1958*, Institute Internationale di Studi Liguri (Bordighera, 1961), which contains accounts of the fine work done by Taillez, Lamboglia, and others. This should be read in order to understand the technical achievements on which our work in Turkey was based.

CHAPTER IV

William Cochran's *Pen and Pencil in Asia Minor* (London, 1887) gives an account of *zeybeks* between Ephesus and Aidin in the 1880's, when they attacked whole towns.

Bodrum: See Newton, in notes to Chapter 1.

CHAPTER V

Diary of Master Thomas Dallan 1599 (Hakluyt Society, London, 1893).

CHAPTER VI

Honor Frost's account of her adventures in Turkey appears in her book, *Under the Mediterranean* (Routledge & Kegan Paul, London, 1963; Prentice-Hall, New York, 1963).

CHAPTER VIII

Most diving manuals give good descriptions of the potential horrors of decompression sickness. The most authoritative is the *United States Navy Diving Manual*, NAVSHIPS 250-538. *The Complete Manual of Free Diving* by Taillez, Dumas, Cousteau *et al.* (G. P. Putnam's Sons, New York, 1957) was the book I used in Turkey. A recent useful book on the subject is *Underwater Medicine*, by Captain Stanley Miles, R.N. (Staples Press, London, 1962).

CHAPTER IX

For a reproduction of the Rekme-Re paintings see *Paintings from the Tomb of Rekh-mi-Re at Thebes*, by Norman de Garies Davies (New York Metropolitan Museum of Art, 1935).

CHAPTER X

Honor Frost's preliminary plans of the Yassi Ada Wrecks II and III are given in her book. The final plan of Wreck III, made by George Bass's crew in 1961 and 1962, together with his preliminary report of the full-scale excavation, is in *Archäologischer Anzeiger*, 1962.

A popular account of the work at Yassi Ada, by George Bass, appeared in the *National Geographic Magazine*, Vol. 124, No. 1, July, 1963.

CHAPTER XI

See my account of the Cochran expedition in the *National Geographic Magazine*, Vol. 117, No. 5, May, 1960, and Stan Waterman's article in *Explorers' Journal*, 38 (1960), No. 3.

The reference from Pliny is cribbed from Beaufort.

CHAPTER XII

The *Adreas* story was told me by several of the participants, years later in Athens. The controversial reference to the village dogs is given on the authority of Captain (now Admiral Ret.) Th. Voutsaras, RHN, who arranged for the salvage ship that brought the welding equipment, and who, with a hired caïque, led the *Adreas* out of the harbor the night of her escape.

CHAPTER XIII

See the bibliography for Chapter X for the Yassi Ada publications.

The reference to Stanko is from Sonnini and Sir John Mandeville, who called it Stanko.

CHAPTER XIV

Europa Minor, Lord Kinross, Patrick Balfour (John Murray, London, 1956). This is a fine account of Kinross's travels in